MOTORCYCLES & MOTORCYCLING in the USSR
USSR
from 1939

A SOCIAL & TECHNICAL HISTORY

COLIN TURBETT

Also from Veloce:

Biographies

A Chequered Life – Graham Warner and the Chequered Flag (Hesletine)
A Life Awheel – The 'auto' biography of W de Forte (Fiction) (Skelton)
Amédée Gordini ... a true racing legend (Smith)
André Lefebvre, and the cars he created at Voisin and Citroën (Beck)
Bunty – Remembering a gentleman of noble Scottish-Irish descent (Schrader)
Chris Carter at Large – Stories from a lifetime in motorcycle racing (Carter & Skelton)
Cliff Allison, The Official Biography of – From the Fells to Ferrari (Gauld)
Edward Turner – The Man Behind the Motorcycles (Clew)
Driven by Desire – The Desiré Wilson Story
First Principles – The Official Biography of Keith Duckworth (Burr)
Inspired to Design – F1 cars, Indycars & racing tyres: the autobiography of Nigel Bennett (Bennett)
Jack Sears, The Official Biography of – Gentleman Jack (Gauld)
Jim Redman – 6 Times World Motorcycle Champion: The Autobiography (Redman)
John Chatham – 'Mr Big Healey' – The Official Biography (Burr)
The Lee Noble Story (Wilkins)
Mason's Motoring Mayhem – Tony Mason's hectic life in motorsport and television (Mason)
Raymond Mays' Magnificent Obsession (Apps)
Pat Moss Carlsson Story, The – Harnessing Horsepower (Turner)
'Sox' – Gary Hocking – the forgotten World Motorcycle Champion (Hughes)
Tony Robinson – The biography of a race mechanic (Wagstaff)
Virgil Exner – Visioneer: The Official Biography of Virgil M Exner Designer Extraordinaire (Grist)

General

BMW Boxer Twins 1970-1995 Bible, The (Falloon)
BMW Cafe Racers (Cloesen)
BMW Custom Motorcycles – Choppers, Cruisers, Bobbers, Trikes & Quads (Cloesen)
Bonjour – Is this Italy? (Turner)
British 250cc Racing Motorcycles (Pereira)
British at Indianapolis, The (Wagstaff)
British Café Racers (Cloesen)
British Cars, The Complete Catalogue of, 1895-1975 (Culshaw & Horrobin)
British Custom Motorcycles – The Brit Chop – choppers, cruisers, bobbers & trikes (Cloesen)
BSA Bantam Bible, The (Henshaw)
BSA Motorcycles – the final evolution (Jones)
Ducati 750 Bible, The (Falloon)
Ducati 750 SS 'round-case' 1974, The Book of the (Falloon)
Ducati 860, 900 and Mille Bible, The (Falloon)
Ducati Monster Bible (New Updated & Revised Edition), The (Falloon)
Ducati Story, The – 6th Edition (Falloon)
Ducati 916 (updated edition) (Falloon)
East German Motor Vehicles in Pictures (Suhr/Weinreich)
Fine Art of the Motorcycle Engine, The (Peirce)
Franklin's Indians (Sucher/Pickering/Diamond/Havelin)
From Crystal Palace to Red Square – A Hapless Biker's Road to Russia (Turner)
Funky Mopeds (Skelton)

The Good, the Mad and the Ugly ... not to mention Jeremy Clarkson (Dron)
Italian Cafe Racers (Cloesen)
Italian Custom Motorcycles (Cloesen)
Kawasaki Triples Bible, The (Walker)
Kawasaki W, H1 & Z – The Big Air-cooled Machines (Long)
Kawasaki Z1 Story, The (Sheehan)
Lambretta Bible, The (Davies)
Laverda Twins & Triples Bible 1968-1986 (Falloon)
Little book of trikes, the (Quellin)
Mike the Bike – Again (Macauley)
Moto Guzzi Sport & Le Mans Bible, The (Falloon)
Moto Guzzi Story, The – 3rd Edition (Falloon)
Motorcycle Apprentice (Cakebread)
Motorcycle GP Racing in the 1960s (Pereira)
Motorcycle Racing with the Continental Circus 1920-1970 (Pereira)
Motorcycle Road & Racing Chassis Designs (Noakes)
Motorcycling in the '50s (Clew)
MV Agusta Fours, The book of the classic (Falloon)
Norton Commando Bible – All models 1968 to 1978 (Henshaw)
Off-Road Giants! (Volume 1) – Heroes of 1960s Motorcycle Sport (Westlake)
Off-Road Giants! (Volume 2) – Heroes of 1960s Motorcycle Sport (Westlake)
Off-Road Giants! (Volume 3) – Heroes of 1960s Motorcycle Sport (Westlake)
Peking to Paris 2007 (Young)
Racing Line – British motorcycle racing in the golden age of the big single (Guntrip)
The Red Baron's Ultimate Ducati Desmo Manual (Cabrera Choclán)
Russian Motor Vehicles – Soviet Limousines 1930-2003 (Kelly)
Russian Motor Vehicles – The Czarist Period 1784 to 1917 (Kelly)
Scooters & Microcars, The A-Z of Popular (Dan)
Scooter Lifestyle (Grainger)
Scooter Mania! – Recollections of the Isle of Man International Scooter Rally (Jackson)
Singer Story: Cars, Commercial Vehicles, Bicycles & Motorcycle (Atkinson)
Speedway – Auto racing's ghost tracks (Collins & Ireland)
Suzuki Motorcycles - The Classic Two-stroke Era (Long)
This Day in Automotive History (Corey)
To Boldly Go – twenty six vehicle designs that dared to be different (Hull)
Triumph Bonneville Bible (59-83) (Henshaw)
Triumph Bonneville!, Save the – The inside story of the Meriden Workers' Co-op (Rosamond)
Triumph Motorcycles & the Meriden Factory (Hancox)
Triumph Speed Twin & Thunderbird Bible (Woolridge)
Triumph Tiger Cub Bible (Estall)
Triumph Trophy Bible (Woolridge)
TT Talking – The TT's most exciting era – As seen by Manx Radio TT's lead commentator 2004-2012 (Lambert)
Velocette Motorcycles – MSS to Thruxton – Third Edition (Burris)
Vespa – The Story of a Cult Classic in Pictures (Uhlig)
Vincent Motorcycles: The Untold Story since 1946 (Guyony & Parker)

Battle Cry!

Soviet General & field rank officer uniforms: 1955 to 1991 (Streather)
Red & Soviet military & paramilitary services: female uniforms 1941-1991 (Streather)

www.veloce.co.uk

First published in February 2019 by Veloce Publishing Limited, Veloce House, Parkway Farm Business Park, Middle Farm Way, Poundbury, Dorchester DT1 3AR, England.
Tel +44 (0)1305 260068 / Fax 01305 250479 / e-mail info@veloce.co.uk / web www.veloce.co.uk or www.velocebooks.com.
ISBN: 978-1-787113-14-5; UPC: 6-36847-01314-1.

MOTORCYCLES & MOTORCYCLING in the
USSR
from 1939

A SOCIAL & TECHNICAL HISTORY

COLIN TURBETT

VELOCE PUBLISHING
THE PUBLISHER OF FINE AUTOMOTIVE BOOKS

CONTENTS

Foreword by Peter J Ballard.. 5

Introduction 6

1. The Great Patriotic War.. 9

2. Postwar factories & models.. 20

3. Exports & evaluations: the view from the UK 45

4. Motorcycle sport in the USSR............................. 55

    Gallery 65

5. Social aspects of motorcycling in the USSR......... 88

Appendix 1: Postwar motorcycle, scooter, moped & cycle motor

production in the USSR 119

Appendix 2: Image sources, bibliography & websites 121

Index...127

FOREWORD
by Peter J Ballard

I bought my first Ural in 1973, a 1971 M63 outfit. Since then I have been fascinated by the history and development of the motorcycles and sidecars from the USSR and the independent countries after the USSR broke up. Much research since has established more of the truth to dispel the many ill-informed myths surrounding Soviet motorcycles – this book helps greatly.

This is a refreshing book as it not only covers the origins, models and specifications of these motorcycles from the early days, but also shows how they were used for work, sport and pleasure in the countries where they were manufactured. This often mirrors how these motorcycles were used in the UK when they first started to appear on our shores in the 1960s, from cheap, utilitarian and rugged transport, to far more of a leisure and indeed 'collectable' motorcycle.

The vast range of photographs included, showing the bikes and sidecars over the decades, is truly fascinating, including many that have not been circulated in print or internet before.

This will be a great read and an excellent resource for those interested in motorcycles out of the ordinary, get out of the shed and read on!

Peter J Ballard
**President of the Cossack Owners'
Club, UK**

INTRODUCTION

Lenin on the Podium by Alexander Gerasimov, 1930. (From *For Soviet Power*)

The Soviet Union (1917-1991) represented an attempt, however distorted it might have eventually become, to create a better world based on values of equality and collective human endeavour. These values were shared and supported by millions of citizens as well as supporters in the West and elsewhere. The fact that this system emerged in opposition to the dominant worldwide one based on market economics and competition, proved to be the USSR's ultimate downfall. Greater Russia at the time of the Revolution in 1917 was a largely backward country dominated by agriculture, and a peasant population who worked on the land. Industry, which was growing at a phenomenal pace in the early years of the 20th century, was concentrated in the hugely expanding cities, like Moscow and St Petersburg (later renamed Leningrad). This included a nascent motorcycle manufacturing industry in Riga and Moscow utilising foreign built engines. The USSR (as Russia and its associated 'Socialist Republics' became known) changed dramatically and violently during its lifetime, and by the end it had achieved incredible levels of scientific advance and industrial output, illustrated by its eminence in the military driven space-race of the 1950s (it was of course soon overtaken by its ideological enemies in the capitalist USA).

Soviet achievements at worst involved the toil – and often took the lives – of the slave labourers of the 'Gulag' – the name popularly given to the system of labour camps in the Soviet Union from the 1930s until the 1950s in which millions were imprisoned. The 'Five Year Plans' of much of the Soviet period drove industrial growth, but at a cost which included the exclusion of freedom of action and thought, and, importantly for the purpose of this book, limited consumer choice and availability of goods for private purchase.

Whilst space technology and some aspects of military hardware were highly advanced, motorcycles remained basic (there were exceptions), and, by comparison with the capitalist countries of the West (and Japan), largely stuck in time. It was only towards the end that serious attempts were made to make Soviet models attractive to consumers, and even then it was mostly cosmetic.

An important feature of Soviet life was the iconography of an emergent nation built on idealism. This found form in the 'socialist realist' school of art and architecture, and was projected internationally through propagandised images of Soviet achievement and the life and work of ordinary citizens. Back at home, people made the best of the opportunities available to them in the new world that emerged after the Great Patriotic War, which had seen victory over Nazi Germany delivered at a human cost that seems overwhelming and beyond imagination. During these postwar years there was a growth in the standard of living and some relative freedom to be enjoyed after Stalin's death in 1953. While in the West motor car ownership became very much associated with economic growth and consumer choice, in the USSR this was reserved for the more privileged in Soviet society. Motorcycles, however, were more accessible, and represented a freedom to move around for a people who were confined to public transport within and between cities, and the horse and cart in rural areas. They were regarded proudly, and looked after and maintained by their owners, who had little recourse to dealers and garages to service or repair their machines. Their use was of course influenced somewhat by the climate, with the harsh Russian winter limiting year-round use throughout much of this vast country, although the state of the roads in rural areas meant they were often more flexible than motor vehicles. They were also used for purposes that seem unusual from a Western perspective, from official parades and circus animal acts, to odd workaday uses for sidecar machines that had largely disappeared in Western Europe by the end of the 1950s.

This book reflects all these features through photographs of motorcycles, their owners and families, the manuals they used to maintain them, associated sport, and officially projected images of motorcycling through the postwar period up until the demise of the Soviet Union in 1991.

Because motorcycling in the USSR was based around quite primitive designs that emerged through the course of the war, the story starts in 1939, with Chapter 1 covering those years and their immediate legacy. As this is the first English language book for many years devoted to Soviet motorcycles of this era, technical details of the principal models (those over 125cc) are described briefly in Chapter 2. Chapter 3 discusses efforts to export Soviet motorcycles to the West which commenced in the 1960s, and Chapter 5 includes a brief examination of the popular models imported to the Soviet Union from other Eastern Bloc countries, notably Czechoslovakia and Hungary. Chapter 4 focuses on motorcycle sport in its various forms as practiced in the Soviet Union.

A prime intention of this book is to capture the social aspect of motorcycling through the Soviet years by way of imagery and iconography – the main focus of the final chapter. The Soviet Union had shortages of most things but not books – they were available in huge numbers from Soviet publishing houses on every subject (so long as they were not officially considered a threat to the state!) and motorcycling was no exception; such manuals and other works are often of high quality (although often cheaply printed) when compared to their equivalents in the West, and so have proved a rich source of material for this book.

A brief word at this point about history and political geography: the text in this book will use the words 'USSR' (Union of Soviet Socialist Republics) and 'Soviet' interchangeably when describing the group of nations that existed from the close of the Russian Civil War of 1919-22, to the end of the ruling regime in 1990/91. At this point the USSR broke up with many former Soviet Republics declaring themselves independent and becoming in all senses, self-governing. The major (and politically dominant) part of the old USSR, the Russian SSR became the new Russian Federation as it exists today. Prior to 1917 the constituent parts of what became the USSR were united under the Russian Tsar, an empire which included Poland. The Russian empire also included Lithuania, Latvia and Estonia, the Baltic States, which gained full independence after 1922. The Baltic States were very controversially absorbed into the USSR in 1939/40, remaining Soviet Republics until the break up of the USSR, and are now in the European Union (EU), the cause of continued political tensions in the region. Other areas of the USSR were always contested, and remain so to this day – the Crimea and Eastern Ukraine being examples. Outside the USSR, after the Soviet victory over Germany of 1945, independent 'Communist' regimes similar (but essentially subservient) to the USSR were established all over Eastern Europe from Eastern Germany (the DDR) in the North to Yugoslavia in the South, and these all severed ties with the Soviet Union from 1989 onwards (Albania and Yugoslavia had already done so). These countries and the USSR were known collectively as the 'Eastern Bloc.'

Finally, this introduction must acknowledge the advice and assistance provided by two very knowledgeable individuals: Peter Ballard from the UK who is President of the Cossack Owners' Club, the home for all who have an interest in the motorcycles described in this book, and Dmitry Larchenko, who is originally from Moscow: Dmitry is a former automotive journalist and now a partner in *Balalaiko*, a Riga, Latvia-based business that renovates Soviet era motorcycles and sells them in other parts of the EU.

Colin Turbett

A Soviet poster from the mid-1930s of Border Guards mounted on a PMZ-A 750cc V Twin. (Author's collection)

КРАСНАЯ АРМИЯ ОПЛОТ МИРНОГО ТРУДА ВЕРНЫЙ СТРАЖ СОВЕТСКИХ ГРАНИЦ

1 THE GREAT PATRIOTIC WAR

"Men make their own history, but they do not make it as they please; they do not make it under self-selected circumstances, but under circumstances existing already, given and transmitted from the past. The tradition of all dead generations weighs like a nightmare on the brains of the living. And just as they seem to be occupied with revolutionizing themselves and things, creating something that did not exist before, precisely in such epochs of revolutionary crisis they anxiously conjure up the spirits of the past to their service, borrowing from them names, battle slogans, and costumes in order to present this new scene in world history in time-honoured disguise and borrowed language."

Karl Marx, *The Eighteenth Brumaire of Louis Bonaparte* (1852).

A book about motorcycles and motorcycling in the USSR can do no worse than start with a quote from Marx, one of the icons of Soviet society. It serves as a useful reminder that postwar life in the Soviet Union was dominated by the memory of World War Two – the 'Great Patriotic War' – when the country came near to defeat, suffering massive destruction and appalling loss of life. The USSR's eventual victory over Nazi Germany was to define subsequent generations, as their rulers sought to make defence and security the main priority – freedom of thought, consumer choice, and spending power coming much further down the list than Cold War competition with the USA and capitalist West.

Motorcycles played a different role in Soviet life than in the West: developed primarily around military requirements, their subsequent civilian history was based on old designs and simplicity of maintenance, so that a home buyer and user might be freer to move about and work than if dependent upon public transport in and between the cities, and horses in the countryside where the road system was primitive at best. Ultimately as consumer choice improved, cheap motor cars were so close in price to motorcycles that development suffered as a consequence, and, through Western eyes at least, what was offered seemed anachronistic and lacking in popular appeal.

By 1939, motorcycles were in mass production in the USSR, simple side-valve and heavy V-twin machines being

Blitzkreig on tow – one horsepower invading German R12 in Gomel, Belarus, 1941. (Author's collection)

Soldier and partisan on a rare and war weary TMZ-53 1000cc-engined M72. (Unknown origin)

produced in factories in Izhevsk in the Urals, Leningrad (now St Petersburg), and Podolsk outside Moscow. By the end of the 1930s, war with an increasingly aggressive Germany looked inevitable, but was successfully sidestepped by the Molotov-Ribbentrop Pact between the two countries in August 1939. This seemed to guarantee non-aggression and territorial division, and therefore avoid war. It also gave the USSR (through a subsequent economic treaty) the benefit of German technology in return for raw materials, grain and oil. Of course, all this changed with the Nazi invasion of Russia in June 1941, and perhaps not unnaturally, the Soviets were less than keen to discuss the detail of the deal thereafter. It seems likely that they did receive plans for BMW's flat-twins that were being mass produced in Bavaria. Russian factory sources however insist that they obtained civilian R71 750cc side-valve bikes for assessment through a third party in Scandinavia in 1940, and subsequently put them into production for military use after evaluation. UK marque expert Peter Ballard (whose article on the subject appeared in Mike Weaver's 2002 book – see Appendix 2) does not believe this, and is certain, from an engineering point of view, that the Russians produced them under licence from BMW. Either way, any evidence seems to have been destroyed during the war. By the time the Germans invaded, M72 motorcycles (as Russia's military version of the German R71 model were known) were in mass production as sidecar hauling machines, and became a mainstay of the Soviet Army throughout the war and beyond. The first

M72s parade in Moscow, October 1941. (Unknown origin)

Female air raid worker and L-300, Moscow 1941. (Author's collection)

military models produced were actually Soviet adaptations of the BMW design, with a bigger engine at 1000cc – the TMZ-53. The manoeuvrability and adaptability of the BMW design rendered them useful for a wide variety of tasks, including as mortar and heavy machine gun mounts.

Development work also commenced for production of a driven sidecar wheel machine, the M73 (as used by the Germans on their overhead valve BMW R75 and Zundapps 750s from 1941), but this seems to have stopped when US-supplied jeeps became more available in about 1943. There is speculation that as sidecar drive was a prewar British invention by the small Baughan manufacturer, the Germans may have been influenced in their very sophisticated design by Norton's crude mechanism, found in captured machines at Dunkirk. However, Zundapp started development on its quite advanced design for the German military as early as 1938, although it was not adopted until the BMW and Zundapp units came into service in 1941.

Alongside the M72, the Soviets used

L-300 convoy to the front, 1941. (Author's collection)

TIZ-AM600 solos on parade. (Unknown origin)

TIZ-AM600 lubrication system.
(From *Motorcycle*, Sytin, B)

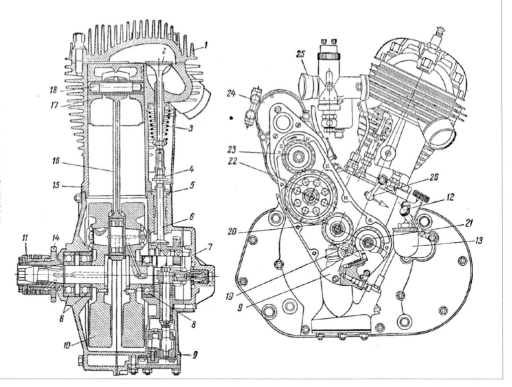

Рис. 11. Четырёхтактный одноцилиндровый двигатель ТИЗ-АМ-600 объёмом 600 см³:

1 — головка цилиндра; 2 — клапан; 3 — пружина клапана; 4 — регулировочный винт; 5 — втулка толкателя; 6 — толкатель; 7 — распределительная коробка; 8 — коренные подшипники; 9 — маслонасос; 10 — маховики; 11 — пружина амортизатора; 12 — маслоуказатель; 13 — патрубок для заливки масла; 14 — цепная звёздочка; 15 — цилиндр; 16 — шатун; 17 — поршень; 18 — поршневой палец; 19 — ведущая шестерня; 20 — шестерня с кулачком впускного клапана; 21 — шестерня с кулачком выпускного клапана; 22 — промежуточная шестерня; 23 — шестерня магдины; 24 — магдина; 25 — карбюратор; 26 — рычажок декомпрессора.

their own L300 200cc two-stroke single machine, a model dating back to 1931, itself based on a German DKW, and built in Leningrad. In the early years of the war they used another DKW copy, the ML-3 125cc two-stroke single, made in Moscow, that was primarily a civilian machine. Later in the war, they used the IZH-350cc two-stroke single, made in Izhevsk, which was a direct copy of the DKW NZ350cc in use with the German army. These last two models, along with the M72, were to form the basis of postwar motorcycle production in the USSR. A fourth home-built machine was the PMZ-A-750, a side-valve V-twin machine not unlike a Harley Davidson, but with a BMW type frame, that was in prewar production in Podolsk. The final Russian

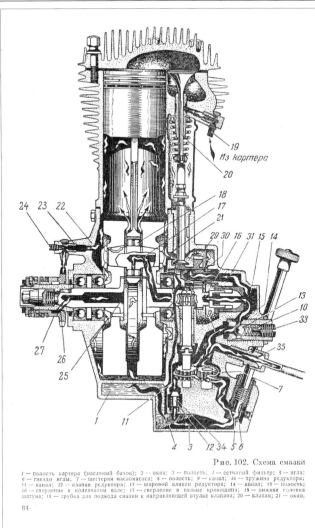

Рис. 102. Схема смазки

1 — полость картера (масляный бачок); 2 — окна; 3 — полость; 4 — сетчатый фильтр; 5 — игла; 6 — гнездо иглы; 7 — шестерни маслонасоса; 8 — полость; 9 — канал; 10 — пружина редуктора; 11 — канал; 12 — клапан редуктора; 13 — шаровой клапан редуктора; 14 — канал; 15 — полость; 16 — сверление в коленчатом валу; 17 — сверление в пальце кривошипа; 18 — нижняя головка шатуна; 19 — трубка для подвода смазки к направляющей втулке клапана; 20 — клапан; 21 — окно,

84

TIZ-AM600 main engine components.

(From *Motorcycle*, Sytin, B)

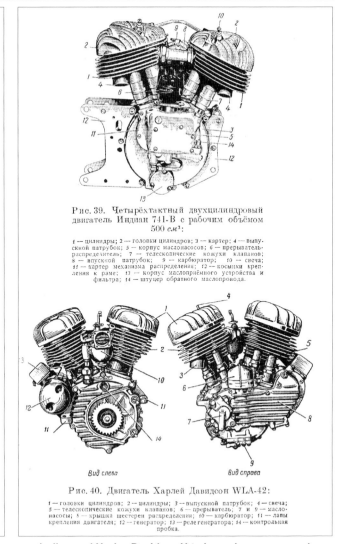

Рис. 39. Четырёхтактный двухцилиндровый двигатель Индиан 741-В с рабочим объёмом 500 см³:

1 — цилиндры; 2 — головки цилиндров; 3 — картер; 4 — выпускной патрубок; 5 — корпус маслонасосов; 6 — прерыватель-распределитель; 7 — телескопические кожухи клапанов; 8 — впускной патрубок; 9 — карбюратор; 10 — свеча; 11 — картер механизма распределения; 12 — косынки крепления к раме; 13 — корпус маслоприёмного устройства и фильтра; 14 — штуцер обратного маслопровода;

Вид слева　　　*Вид справа*

Рис. 40. Двигатель Харлей Давидсон WLA-42:

1 — головки цилиндров; 2 — цилиндры; 3 — выпускной патрубок; 4 — свеча; 5 — телескопические кожухи клапанов; 6 — прерыватель; 7 и 9 — масло-насосы; 8 — крышка шестерен распределения; 10 — карбюратор; 11 — лапы крепления двигателя; 12 — генератор; 13 — реле генератора; 14 — контрольная пробка.

Indian and Harley Davidson V-twin engines compared.

(From *Motorcycle*, Sytin, B)

model in extensive use was the TIZ-AM-600 side-valve single, a 1936 model clearly based on the 1931 BSA Sloper model, and made latterly in Tyumen in the Urals.

After the Nazi invasion the Soviet Union quickly aligned itself with the Allies, and, along with other military supplies, received numerous motorcycles that were in use with the British and US armies. These included over 30,000 Harley and Indian V-twins, Ariel WNG 350cc OHV singles, Norton 16H 500cc side-valve singles, Matchless G3 350cc OHV singles, BSA M20 500cc side-valve singles, and Velocette MAF 350cc OHV singles. The accompanying illustrations suggest that many of these must have been around after the war had

finished, but none, it seems, influenced Soviet postwar design and production to the same extent as those that came from the defeated Germans.

The Great Patriotic War ranged far and wide across the enormity of Western Russia for three years, until the Soviet armies finally pushed the Germans beyond their borders in 1944, and all the way to the heart of the beast, Berlin, in the spring of 1945. During this time tens of millions of soldiers and civilians died, and the country was laid waste. In the ebbs and flows of battle, losses included vast amounts of equipment; the military effort was only maintained because of the wholescale removal east to the Urals, and

Harley Davidson WLA 45 and rider, Major Alexei Fidyukov, 2nd Ukrainian Front, 1945. (Author's collection)

beyond to Siberia, of industrial production, including motorcycle manufacture. Battle zones ranged from the Arctic North to the Black Sea, and the Far East in the short campaign against Japan in mid-1945. Most of the fronts where the main armies fought it out involved a requirement for mobility, and the Red Army found motorcycles very useful in all climates and conditions – a lesson that was to ensure their continued military purpose, and guarantee high levels of production in the postwar years.

In 1945 Eastern Germany lay in the Soviet-dominated sector, and, in the chaos that followed defeat, the DKW factory at Zschopau was plundered; everything of value (including some personnel) was taken back to the USSR. This, of course, kick-started the postwar production of DKW 125cc lookalike bikes, as we shall see in Chapter 2. The Soviets were not alone in this: BSA in the United Kingdom did exactly the same with its postwar Bantam 125cc, which, like the Russian variant, continued

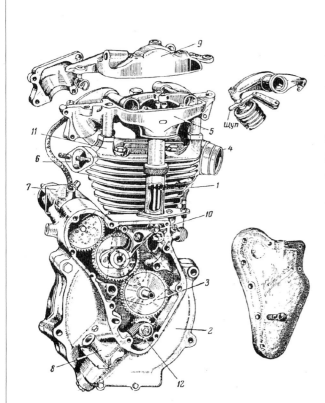

Рис. 35. Четырёхтактный одноцилиндровый двигатель Велосетт МАF-350 с рабочим объёмом 350 см³:

1 — цилиндр; 2 — картер; 3 — шестерни газораспределения; 4 — выпускной патрубок; 5 — коробка коромысел; 6 — впускной патрубок; 7 — магнето; 8 — прилив под корпус маслонасоса; 9 — крышка коробки коромысел; 10 — роккеры; 11 — головка цилиндра; 12 — полуось коленчатого вала.

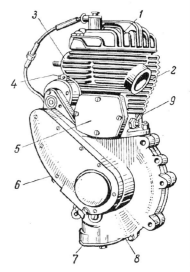

Рис. 36. Четырёхтактный одноцилиндровый двигатель BSA M-20 с рабочим объёмом 500 см³:

1 — головка цилиндра; 2 — выпускной патрубок; 3 — впускной патрубок; 4 — магдина; 5 — крышка распределительного механизма; 6 — крышка распределительных шестерён; 7 — маслонасос; 8 — картер; 9 — цилиндр.

British Velocette MAF and BSA M20 engines explained to the Red Army. (From *Motorcycle*, Sytin, B)

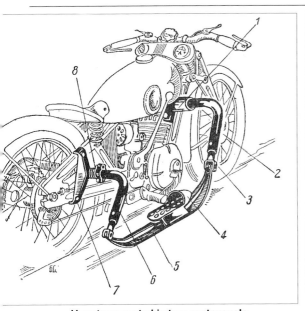

How to mount skis to a motorcycle.
(From *Motorcycle*, Sytin, B)

Ski-equipped TIZ-AM600. (Author's collection)

German troops inspect damaged and abandoned Red Army motorcycles, Pskov. (Unknown origin)

How to dress to ride a Velocette MAF 350cc.

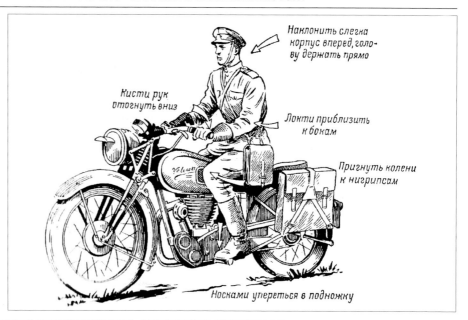

Наклонить слегка корпус вперед, голо-ву держать прямо

Кисти рук отогнуть вниз

Локти приблизить к бокам

Пригнуть колени к нигрипсам

Носками упереться в подножку

How to ride at speed ...

... and how to corner.

The correct distance for safe group riding. (All images on this page from *Motorcycle*, Sytin, B)

An M72 rider
defends against air
attack.
(Unknown origin)

Red Army
troops inspect
captured NSU
350 motorcycles.
(Unknown origin)

in production for several decades. In the USA, Harley Davidson, too, produced its own version of this cheap and easily produced utility machine. A similar plunder took place at the BMW plants in Spandau (Berlin) and Eisenach, that also fell into the hands of the Red Army. To the victors the spoils – and Soviet officers helped themselves to German machines for their own use, just as their masters extracted

Trying to fix a captured German Triumph SK250 from the early 1930s. (Author's collection)

A BMW R25 250cc receives attention from a Soviet officer, 1945. (Author's collection)

Red army soldier Boris Ignatovich on a captured BMW R25 250cc. (Unknown origin)

A Red Army officer poses on an NSU, 1945. (Author's collection)

A studio photo of a decorated Soviet soldier mounted on a Brennabor motorcycle. (Author's collection)

reparations for the awful damage wreaked by the German armies in Russia.

For the armies the war was over – but was it? Soon the 'Cold War' against the West became a dominant feature in Soviet life, guaranteeing continued high levels of military spending, and consequent hard times for the beleaguered survivors of the real war against Germany and its allies. The priority was to rebuild the devastated west of the USSR, and hardship would continue for many years. Motorcycling would have its place in the country's future but funds for innovation and development as an industry were simply not available. It was time to fall back on what was readily to hand.

The Soviet Army Monument, Sofia, Bulgaria. (From *War Memorials*)

Soviet officers pose with a civilian NSU in Vienna after war's end. (Author's collection)

Soviet officers on a captured Zundapp outfit, Germany, late 1945. (Author's collection)

Red Army women with an M72, Vienna, July 1945. (Author's collection)

2 POSTWAR FACTORIES & MODELS

INTRODUCTION

The USSR that emerged victorious from the Great Patriotic War in 1945 was a greatly depleted nation, despite gains in territory through military conquest.

Although estimated numbers are disputed, official 1993 Russian Government figures suggest that over 26 million Soviet citizens, mostly men, lost their lives. Western Russia, Ukraine and Byelorussia, the scenes of great battles and deliberate destruction over the previous four years, were devastated beyond imagination. Food production was decimated in these war zones, and for many years huge numbers of survivors eked out a meagre living in dugouts in the ground. Industry throughout the USSR was depleted by 25% of prewar production levels (Hobsbawm, 1994) with priority given to armaments. In several territories that had been occupied by the Nazis there were also insurgencies requiring ongoing military action for several years. The priority for Stalin's administration was stability (involving further rounds of terror until his death in 1953) and the rebuilding of industry, housing and agriculture. Such issues were gradually tackled at the same time as the USSR engaged in continued military spending to maintain its place as a great power. Motorcycle production, initially (and importantly) as cheap transport for the masses, was gradually extended: by the 1960s, exports had begun and models were being produced around leisure and not just functional need.

In the popular imagination, Soviet era motorcycles are seen as old-fashioned copies of prewar German models – cheaply made and of poor quality. However, to put this in context, motorcycle production in Britain, which declined throughout the period under description (when USSR output increased year on year) was also based on outdated models and (arguably) dubious quality that fell prey eventually to Japanese innovation, flair and engineering skill. The most popular British motorcycle export to the USA in the 1950s and 1960s was the Triumph Twin, a design that went back to 1938; the biggest selling British model of all time (1946-1970) was the BSA Bantam – a mirror image copy of the prewar German DKW R125 – just like the Soviet M1A and its descendants. As we shall see, the USSR developed its basic range considerably over the years, and also produced racing machinery (described in Chapter 4) as exotic as anything produced at the time in Italy or elsewhere..

This chapter will describe standard production, and development in the USSR, starting with an overview of the manufacturing facilities, and go on to describe the various standard models. There were, as we shall see, fundamental issues affecting motorcycle production and use in the USSR, including the availability of some items taken for granted in Europe and the West, such as good quality oil. Servicing facilities were also almost non-existent, and the buyer and rider was expected to make and mend on the basis of his or her own initiative. Bikes were sold through state outlets, but 'customer care' was unheard of: new bikes arrived in their packaging, and it was up to the new owner to unwrap and assemble them. In the cities, where housing during most of the Soviet years was in short supply due to rapid expansion, accommodation was very basic, often involving shared facilities for cooking and washing. There was no garaging for motorcycles, and, because they were valued so highly, great effort was made to look after them. Roads in rural areas were poor, with consequent

wear and tear issues. Motorcycles, though, as we shall see in Chapter 5, were very popular.

THE FACTORIES

In the USSR production was, in theory at least, centrally planned through various government ministries. The establishment of a plant in a particular city was supposed to be part of a wider plan rather than the result of local initiative. Central planning would be based on considerations such as the availability of labour, raw materials and transport, but would also set targets for production based on projected need – resulting in an emphasis on quantity rather than quality. In the USSR motorcycle factories were typically quite self-contained, tending to make a lot of their own components, and were not so dependent on a supply chain as was, for example the British motorcycle industry in relation to electrical components. This explains how, despite central planning, each factory developed the centrally agreed models in its own way, with its own designers and technicians. Important changes, though, were the result of ministerial decree at the highest level. The plan for motorcycle production developed in the early 1950s determined that Kiev and Irbit would make the larger flat-twin machines, Izhevsk the 350cc two-strokes, Kovrov, 125cc and 175cc two-strokes, and Minsk, 125cc two-strokes. Other plants were designated to produce the smaller capacity scooters, mopeds and cycle motors (these are not detailed in this book but are included in the model chart in Appendix 1). Their locations are shown alongside the large scale factories in the map on the next page, along with the Tyumen factory, whose short history really pre-dates this survey.

This is not the place to discuss the planning of the economy in detail, but the process changed from a heavily centralised and chaotic one during Stalin's time (he died in 1953), to a theoretically more efficient one, based on local factors during the Khrushchev years of the late 1950s and early 1960s. An anecdotal, but no doubt truth-based story from the

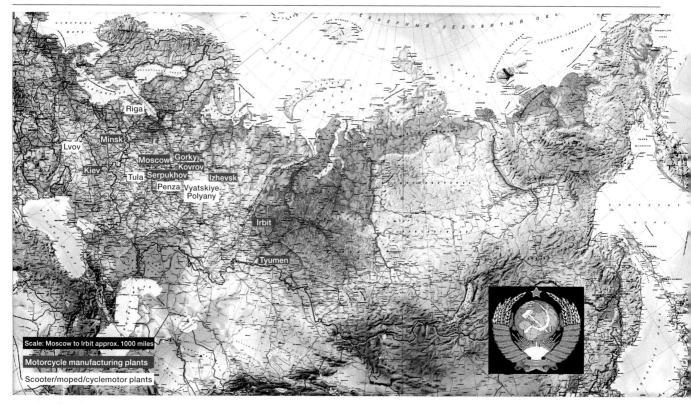

Map showing location of wartime and postwar motorcycle plants in the USSR.

1950s, quoted by historian Moshe Lewin, concerns two factories in Kazan, one of which needed a component made by the other; this required contact with Moscow who then authorised delivery of the parts needed, in a special train from the capital 500 miles away – even though there were stocks just along the road! Planning was further reformed in later years, but never achieved anything approaching perfection, and the whole economy went into decline in the 1980s. Waste and inefficiency were traits that affected motorcycle production until the end of the Soviet era. Receptions and parties were commonplace, and their purpose dubious. Lewin quotes one factory in Izhevsk (he does not state whether this was the large armaments plant that also produced motorcycles, but it might well have been) draining 650 bottles of cognac, 25 bottles of vodka, and 80 bottles of champagne between October 1967 and July 1968. The English motorcycle importer Nev Mason, who worked on development with the Minsk and Kiev factories, refers to such merrymaking in his memoirs. The dual nature of the Soviet economy in its

later years of decline is also illustrated by car and motorcycle servicing – an area almost entirely relegated to the non-state sector, where tax was avoided and services paid for by cash or the barter of black-market goods. Some examples of production inefficiencies will be found in the narrative below. However, motorcycle production in the USSR, in whatever way it might be viewed, must at least be compared favourably with the UK where it almost disappeared during those same years.

Gorky – GMZ

The factory in Gorky (a city now known as Nizhny Novgorod) was established in 1941 to manufacture military M72 motorcycles. According to a Ukrainian internet source (http://www.motodrive. com) production was moved, along with all plant and machinery, from Kharkov and Leningrad, both of which were threatened with German occupation. By 1950-51, production had again been relocated, along with about 100 employees, to Kiev, with some workers going to the Serpukhov plant.

Wartime M72 production. (Unknown origin)

Irbit – IMZ

Motorcycle manufacturing in Irbit, east of the Ural Mountains, owes its development to the wartime move, east and away from the conflict zones, of much Soviet manufacturing capacity in the early years of the Great Patriotic War. In 1941 a decision was made to relocate military motorcycle production, as described elsewhere in this section. The Moscow motorcycle production unit was transplanted to Irbit in the Ural Mountains region. A former brewery site was converted into a research and development facility to pave the way for the creation of a large factory that would be devoted to M72 motorcycle production. This all happened quickly, thanks to the relentless toil of the construction workforce, and the first machines were sent to the front in October 1942. Between then and the end of the war, 9799 M72 motorcycles were produced. After the war, the plant was expanded to continue M72 production for the military, and in 1954 it went over to civilian production. In 1957 all the tooling for the M72 was sold to China (including, it is reputed, some original BMW equipment) where M72 production (as the M1) continues to this day under the 'Chang Jiang' brand name. Meanwhile, the Irbit plant changed to output of OHV flat-twin motorcycles, later sold under the 'Ural' and 'Mars' brand names. These were subject to development as the years went by, and are still in production today. At the beginning of the 1980s, a village next to the factory was demolished to make way for development that would increase output to 200,000 machines a year. However, this was dropped as a consequence of the economic stagnation of that decade that ended with 'perestroika' and the ditching of the Soviet system. Irbit's post-Soviet history is all about the capitalist style of enterprise that dominates the Russian economy

The Irbit factory decorated with 'Order of Symbol of Honour' award. (Unknown origin)

today: in 2000 it was bought by a group of US-based Russian-born entrepreneurs, who moved its base to Seattle, USA, and proceeded to build that country as its prime market. They also reorganised the plant by drastically reducing its size and workforce, and buying in components from across the world. Irbit is something of a Mecca for Russian motorcycle devotees, and hosts a large rally in July of every year.

Izhevsk – IZH

The giant Izhevsk (sometimes spelt 'Ishevsk' in translation to English) manufacturing complex, was already well established when motorcycle production began in 1928. This continued until 1940 with steady development of models, until the war dictated total focus on arms manufacturing, with relocation from other parts of the Western USSR threatened by the German invasion. The plant is perhaps better known for small arms manufacturing, at one time being the main supplier of arms to the Red Army, its output including the Kalashnikov (AK47) machine gun. Postwar

Workers housing in Izhevsk. (Author's collection)

Factory sports ground Izhevsk. (Author's collection)

The Izhevsk factory, from a 1989 publicity brochure. (Author's collection)

Izhevsk motorcycle production 1989. (Author's collection)

production of the DKW-like IZH 350 two-stroke single commenced in 1947, and development of that basic model continued for many years. From the early 1960s the plant produced 350cc single two-stroke machines under the 'Planeta' name, and 350cc twins under the 'Jupiter' name. Modern mass production techniques prevailed at Izhevsk, the biggest volume motorcycle producer in the Soviet Union: the one millionth motorcycle being made in 1960, two millionth in 1965, three million by 1972, and four million by the mid-1980s. The factory also produced cars and vans from 1966 onwards, and changed its name from the Izhevsk Machine Building Plant to Izhmash Industrial Association in 1974. The factory continues in production to this day as the 'Kalashnikov Concern,' but motorcycle manufacture ended in 2008.

Kiev – KMZ

Kiev, the capital of the Ukrainian Soviet Socialist Republic between 1921 and 1991 (and now capital of independent Ukraine), was virtually flattened during the war. However, development

and production of small capacity civilian motorcycles (the K-1B 98cc) commenced there in 1945 on the site of an armoured car and tank repair base. The first K-1B appeared in 1946 with an engine produced in the Moscow factory, but by 1947 complete bikes were being manufactured. Also prioritised for production in the Kiev (KMZ) factory at this time was the K-1V, a simple motorcycle-based three-wheeled invalid carriage, the 'Invalidka,' designed for the Soviet Union's very large number of war disabled veterans, a common sight on the streets of every city in the USSR until the 1990s. In 1951, production of the K-1B was ended, and the K-1V transferred to Serpukhov (where it became the S-1V and was subsequently developed into a proper enclosed vehicle). In 1950, KMZ became the centre of production for military M72 motorcycles which had (from 1941) centred on Gorky. Initially the Kiev factory used frames supplied from Irbit. The production of civilian machines commenced in 1958 with the development of the overhead valve (OHV) 500cc M53, only produced in very small numbers, and civilian versions of the M72. OHV flat-twins of 650cc capacity (actually 649cc) subsequently appeared and these, along with the side-valve K750cc, became the mainstay of production by KMZ, using the 'Dnepr' (sometimes spelt 'Dnieper' in English) brand, named after the River that runs through Kiev. KMZ's millionth motorcycle produced was celebrated in 1979, and the two millionth ten years later.

The Kiev plant was a massive affair covering a large area. It always focused on motorcycle production, but in the 1960s experimented with production of four wheel 'motorloaders' (the type of vehicle that might be used internally within a large factory), stationary engines, and a fire-fighting sidecar outfit. It also produced a successful two-stroke racer, the SSH-500 in the 1970s, and experimental transverse V-twins and Wankel-engined motorcycles through into the 1980s. Over the years it retooled and modernised, constantly increasing its output, reaching 45-50,000 units per year between 1955 and 1970. Particular care was given to components for military use, which were checked carefully, and given a 'red star' or other marks if of sufficient quality.

Kovrov – ZID

The Degtyaryov Plant was established in the city of Kovrov in 1916 for the manufacture of armaments, and has been doing so ever since. In 1946,

the USSR automotive ministry decreed that the plant would produce 125cc two-stroke single motorcycles using plans and machinery, taken as war reparations from the DKW Zschopau factory in Germany, to make the K125 model. Some 279 machines were produced in 1946. The K125 was developed and produced until 1960, when production of this capacity model ceased. By this time, production output had reached a million machines.

Meantime, in 1957, a larger two-stroke 175cc single model started in production, and became the mainstay of the factory through to the end of the Soviet era, enjoying steady development under the 'Voskhod' model name from 1963. By the 1970s, 220,000 bikes a year were coming out of Kovrev. The factory also produced

road racers and other sports bikes. The plant is still in production, turning out small capacity motorcycles in conjunction with the Chinese Lifan company, as well as armaments.

Moscow – MMZ (until 1951)

The Moscow plant was established in 1941 to manufacture military M72 motorcycles, but soon moved to Irbit due to the threats to production posed by the Nazi invasion. In 1946, the plant went back into production on the basis of plans and machinery transferred as war reparations from the DKW factory in Zschopau Germany (as with Kovrov), making M1A 125cc motorcycles alongside bicycles. In 1951, motorcycle production was transferred to Minsk.

'Wheels for the Workers.' Advertisement for the Moscow factory. (*Ogonek*, No 26, 1949 – Russian magazine)

Moscow motorcycle production in 1947. (*Ogonek*)

Minsk – MMZ (from 1951)

The Minsk factory in the Byelorussian Soviet Socialist Republic's capital (now the capital of independent Belarus) was established in 1951 under decree 494 of

The Minsk factory, 1953. (*Soviet Union* – English language magazine published in Moscow)

the USSR Automotive Ministry to take over production of the M1A 125cc motorcycle – an exact copy of the German DKW 125cc two-stroke single. 125cc production became the mainstay of the plant throughout the Soviet period, the basic design being considerably developed over the years, produced in millions and exported worldwide. The factory continues in production today, under private ownership since 2007.

Serpukhov – SMZ

The factory complex in Serpukhov, about 90 kilometres south of Moscow, was converted from a NKVD young offenders colony in 1939 and began production of ML3 125cc two-stroke singles in 1940. This ceased at the start of the war, and the works went over to the repair of military motorcycles, including the large number of US and British machines that were sent to the USSR. Postwar, the factory was used for many purposes including, notably, as an all-USSR research and development institute: in the 1950s and '60s, specialist racing motorcycles were developed at Serpukhov. In 1951 the plant also began making invalid vehicles after transfer of production from Kiev, and continued to develop and make these into the 1990s.

Towards the end of the Soviet era, the factory produced a very small number (said to be 50) of Dnepr-based overhead valve flat-twins known as 'The Kremlin Escort' – an expensive specification with high-performance parts and speed to match. Sold off into private hands in the post-USSR period, the plant, by then known as SeAZ and manufacturing cars, was declared bankrupt in 2013.

Tyumen – TMZ

The short-lived Tyumen plant is mentioned here for completeness, although it pre-dates this postwar survey. Its location in Western Siberia (about 120 miles east of Irbit), was based on the resiting in 1941 of the Taganrog plant (TIZ) from south-western Russia, which had produced the TIZ AM-600 motorcycle in the years preceding the war. Tyumen's planned purpose was to produce M72s alongside AM-600s. However, according to b-cozz. com (a useful web-based archive of information on Russian motorcycles) this never fully materialised, and only 614 AM-600 machines had been assembled before parts dried up in 1943, when equipment and workforce were moved to Gorky. M72 production had not commenced by then, although the factory did develop the TMZ-53 – a 1000cc side-valve boxer twin with a new frame and driven sidecar wheel.

THE MODELS

The motorcycles made in the various factories described above are most simply described in their family groups. Postwar there were three basic designs of Soviet motorcycle (I exclude here the Scooters and smaller machines of less than 100cc capacity which are not described in this book). These were: the 125cc two-stroke singles based on the German DKW, the 350cc two-stroke singles based on the DKW NZ model, and the 750cc large side-valve flat-twins based on BMW designs. Out of these emerged other Soviet-designed machines, including 175cc two-stroke singles, 350cc two-stroke twins (emulating the very successful Czech Jawa designs) and overhead valve flat-twins of 650cc (649cc, but I will refer to them in the text as 650cc), and those of larger 750cc capacity. Others were experimented with along the way, but never went into volume production. The standard models will be briefly described here, whilst the sports models will be covered in a later chapter. The table provided in Appendix 1 gives detail of all powered two-wheeled volume production (not those made for competition and racing), so the extent of this can be seen. Some photos of smaller models that are not covered here

are included in Chapter 5, which looks at the social aspect of motorcycling in the Soviet Union.

The 125cc two-stroke singles

In 1945 Zschopau, the site of a large DKW motorcycle factory in eastern Germany, was in the hands of the conquering Red Army. Apparently, whether or not as official war

Russian Moskva 125 c.c. two-stroke, which is a German D.K.W. under another name

Moskva M1A 125cc in *The Motor Cycle*, 10th Feb, 1949.
(© Morton's Media)

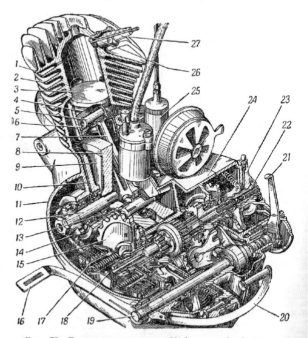

Рис. 73. Двигатель мотоцикла М1А с коробкой передач:
1—головка цилиндра; *2*—цилиндр; *3*—поршень; *4*—компрессионное поршневое кольцо; *5*—поршневой палец; *6*—стопорное кольцо; *7*—шатун; *8*—щека кривошипа; *9*—крышка щеки кривошипа; *10*—левая половина картера; *11*—левая крышка картера; *12*—левая цапфа кривошипа; *13*—палец кривошипа; *14*—ведущая звездочка; *15*—ведомая звездочка; *16*—педаль переключения передач; *17*—сцепление; *18*—грибок штока выключения сцепления; *19*—валик переключения передач; *20*—рычаг пускового механизма; *21*—стрелка указателя передач; *22*—червяк выключения сцепления; *23*—правая крышка картера; *24*—правая половина картера; *25*—карбюратор; *26*—отверстие для декомпрессора; *27*—запальная свеча

M1A main components. (*Motorcycle Design*)

reparations, the factory, which had largely evaded allied bombing, was stripped bare and everything transported back to the USSR. Given the terrible damage inflicted on the Soviet Union by the Nazis few would question the morality of this. After the war the site was taken over and used as a motorcycle plant again, starting almost from scratch, producing first IFA and then MZ motorcycles (including the world beating two-strokes, whose stolen technology was to launch Japanese racing successes in the 1960s and 1970s). As a result of this transfer of technology to the USSR, high level decisions were quickly made to the take the small 125cc DKW into Soviet production as the Moskva M1A in Moscow, and as the Komet K125 in Kovrov. This was a simple design also adopted by the British as the BSA Bantam, as well as Harley Davidson in the USA, WFM in Poland and (later) Yamaha in Japan. It was intended to be a mass-produced machine that would help workers get around, and boost an economy that lay in tatters, and in that purpose it was successful. Both the M1A and K125 had a rigid frame and pressed steel girder forks, which were changed to basic telescopic ones in 1952. By 1951 the Moscow production had transferred to

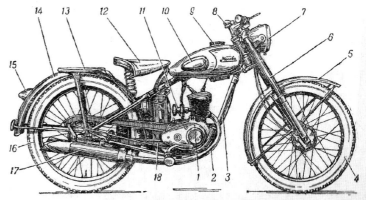

Рис. 4. Мотоцикл М1А (общий вид):
1—двигатель с коробкой передач; 2—выпускная труба; 3—рама; 4—переднее колесо; 5—передний щиток; 6—передняя вилка; 7—фара; 8—маховичок рулевого амортизатора; 9—пробка бензинового бака; 10—резиновая подушка; 11—карбюратор; 12—седло водителя; 13—багажник; 14—задний щиток; 15—задний фонарь; 16—заднее колесо; 17—глушитель; 18—щиток цепи главной передачи

M1A engine. (*Motorcycle Design*)

Minsk. Sports varieties were produced by the factories from the earliest years. The early Kovrov and Moscow/Minsk models differed only in finish, but their subsequent developed forms began to take their own individual form with differing electrical systems and clutch design.

In 1956 Kovrov introduced a swinging arm version of the 125cc – the K55, and this was refined into the K58 in 1958, lasting a further two years until 1960. The K58 had a slight increase in power, improved lighting,

An original Moskva from 1954, shown at the UK Stafford Show, April 2018. (Author)

Komet K125 in 1953. (Author's collection)

K55. (*K125 and K175 Motorcycles*)

Рис. 3. Дорожный мотоцикл К-55

M101, 1960. (Avtoexport)

a toolbox, and the distinctively shaped Kovrov petrol tank, that was to grace other models with its metal hare motifs. It also had an alternator electrical system that allowed starting without reliance on the battery – a bonus in those times. This was to be the final Kovrov 125cc, production from then on being concentrated in Minsk.

The Minsk swinging arm 125cc appeared in 1958 as the M101, with an increase in power over the original engine from 4.75 to 5.00bhp, and enjoyed similar upgrades to its Kovrov-made equivalent. Very slight modifications were made with the introduction of the M103 model in 1961, the two being produced together until 1964. A more thorough revamp and modernisation to make it more attractive to buyers came in 1965 with the introduction of the M104, which had a dual seat, enclosed panels on each side, and a cover to the carburettor. Power output, though, remained the same. A significant power increase to 7bhp, brought about through collaboration with the MZ factory in Zschopau, occurred with the M105 and M106 models that were produced from 1969 to 1974 (the M106 from 1971). MZ, influenced by the racing successes brought about by its engineer Walter Kaaden, was in the forefront of two-stroke technology at that time. This power increase was enhanced through a four-speed gearbox. Looks remained much as they were, the bike's emphasis being on robustness and reliability rather than power and speed. Rather more thorough refinement and modernisation of the model came about in 1974 with the Minsk 125 model. This again was

Minsk 125, 1975. (*Za Rulem*, Russian magazine)

the result of collaboration with MZ, and enjoyed more modern looks, better brakes, bigger wheels, and a further power increase to 8bhp achieved through engine modifications including the use of lighter material for the cylinder. This bike became a firm favourite, both at home and abroad, and achieved massive sales – running into the millions by the end of the Soviet period. One of the biggest importers of the Minsk 125cc bikes was Vietnam, where they enjoy a following to this day – a rally attended by thousands taking place annually.

This was not the end of the story: from about 1976 Minsk introduced the 11bhp MMVZ 3-115 variant, with a Sports version, the MMVZ 3-115S, to be followed in 1982 by the 12bhp MMVZ 3.112 with stronger chassis parts for more robust road use. These bikes had contactless electronic ignition, indicators, and other refinements. The sports model had street-enduro looks with a high-level exhaust and rev counter. These bikes were heavier than the former, and were more basic models, but could achieve 95km/h – some 5km/h more than the Minsk 125, 10km/h more than the M105/M106 and 25km/h more than the original M1A!

The 175cc two-stroke singles

The Kovrov-produced 175cc single cylinder motorcycles were direct developments of the 125cc DKW-derived motorcycles described above. The factory engineers

simply created a larger bore cylinder and placed it on the same engine base, to create the K175, an 8bhp machine, in 1957. The bike's power unit, driven through three gears, was crude, but the frame was enlarged after the first 400 oversized 125cc machines were made, giving way to a modern look that appealed to buyers. In subsequent years the wheel size was reduced from 19 to 16 inches in diameter, which also enhanced the bike's appearance. In 1959, engine development for the K175A allowed for four gears, but still with the same power output, and also featured an improved front fork design. A further update occurred in 1962 with the K175B model, which increased power

MMVZ 3111, 1972.
(Avtoexport)

K175, 1960.
(Avtoexport)

and lowered fuel consumption with a new carburettor. However, flaws in the design and materials used resulted in heavy wear and early-life engine problems, so the model only lasted for a year. A complete revamp of the 175 took place with the launch of the Voskhod series in 1963. This took forward the concept, with styling that enhanced the attractive looks of the Kovrovets, along with improved suspension and speedometer, a rear rack, side mirror, and, for export models, knee guards and windscreen. Power was increased to 10bhp and top speed to 85km/h or 90 with tuned engine. This model lasted through the '60s, until replacement by the Voskhod 2 in 1970, which evidenced continued improvement, including indicators and styling, power increase and, from 1976, contactless ignition. The 2M version, launched in 1977, was capable of 100km/h. The model enjoyed further refinement with the introduction of the Voskhod 3 series in 1980. This was a far more western looking bike, combining Kovrov styling with an export market appeal, and, from 1983, 12-volt electrics. The Voskhod 3 had rear shock absorbers that could be adjusted for height, a modern instrument console and twin ports. Power peaked now at 14bhp, giving a top speed of 105km/h – not bad for a 175! The Voskhod 3 was produced until 1989 when production at this capacity was ended in the USSR. Other developments were said to be in progress in the 1970s and 1980s, including a powerful 250cc, but this was not to be. The Kovrov machines were cheap and popular, and explanations for their demise are varied. One suggestion was the need to increase armament production at Kovrov, in the light of the Afghan war; another was that ministerial favour went to Izhevsk and that this reduced competition.

The 350cc four-stroke single

Although it never went into production, the M31 motorcycle is mentioned here because it was the only postwar four-stroke single developed in the Soviet Union. Designed at Serpukhov in 1954 at the bequest of the Minsk plant, it bears a resemblance to the East German AWO 425

M31 350cc. (Unknown origin)

250cc, and also had a modern swinging arm frame and shaft drive, but was a unique design and heavier, at 160kg. Its lines and cradle frame remind one of the larger British Norton Featherbed twins of that era, and it was certainly advanced with power output of 18bhp and 110km/h capability. However the central planners had already determined that Minsk would produce smaller capacity bikes, and so the project was abandoned.

The 350cc two-stroke singles

At the end of the war in 1945, experts were apparently sent from Izhevsk to Germany, returning (as war reparations) with technical plans, DKW chief designer Hermann Weber, and machinery sufficient to produce up to 35,000 DKW NZ 350cc motorcycles a year. According to information on the b-cozz.com website, the director of the plant exhorted the Izhevsk workforce to simply copy the German model, and not to bother with any ideas of their own, as the plant's expertise at that time lay in arms production. The result – the IZH 350 was, as can be seen in the illustrations, an exact replica. The bike enjoyed a rugged simplicity, but also proven German quality in design that had made it popular with German despatch riders during the war. With pressed steel girder forks, rigid rear end, hand-change four-speed gears, and twin ports, it was a great success in the Soviet Union: 126,297 being produced between 1947 and 1951, filling at least some of the need for basic transportation. The bike reached 11.5bhp, and was capable of a speed of 90km/h.

In 1951, the basic 350 was replaced by

the IZH 49. This had an identical engine, but greatly improved chassis, with plunger-type rear suspension, telescopic forks, and better comfort. During the next four years, over half a million of these models were built, more than any other motorcycle produced in the world at that time, to a quality that was generally regarded as high. It was also offered with a sidecar option. The IZH 49 continued in production until 1958, but its replacement, the IZH 56, was introduced in 1956. This altered the looks of the basic 350 in favour of a modern swinging arm framed bike with a dual seat, chrome, and general styling to enhance its attraction. Engine improvements increased power to 13bhp, boosting top speed to 100km/h.

The replacement for the IZH 56 did not enter volume production until 1961, and was known as the 'Planeta,' a model name that was to feature for many years to come. The first Planeta models were very similar in styling to the 1956 model, but with an improved air filter to give longer engine life, and some minor detail changes, but the Planeta 2, in 1966, brought in engine improvement and an increase in power to 15.5bhp. Output for these bikes exceeded over half a million examples. It had been intended that the single cylinder bikes would be dropped in favour of the new and more powerful 350cc twins (see below), but sales figures for the latter did not meet expectations, and the two lines were developed alongside one another.

More significant changes and modernisation occurred with the introduction of the Planeta 3 in 1971. This brought in a new shape of petrol tank, improved electrics (including indicators), and engine power increase to 18bhp, giving a top speed of 110km/h. The look was not unlike some of the early popular Japanese machines of the same capacity, and was therefore attractive to foreign markets (especially with its low cost), and an audience of young people in the USSR itself.

In 1974 the trend for market satisfaction, especially amongst young people, took a new turn with the 'Planeta Sport' model. This single port and attractively-styled bike was a match for western rivals. Developed from competition models

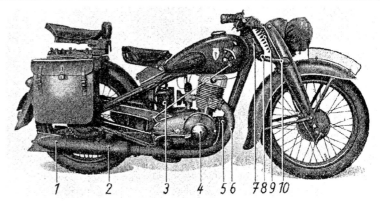

Wartime DKW NZ 350cc. (Author's collection)

IZH49 350cc. (Author's collection)

IZH 350. (Author's collection)

IZH Planeta, 1960.
(Avtoexport)

IZH Planeta 3
advert. (*Za Rulem*,
April 1970)

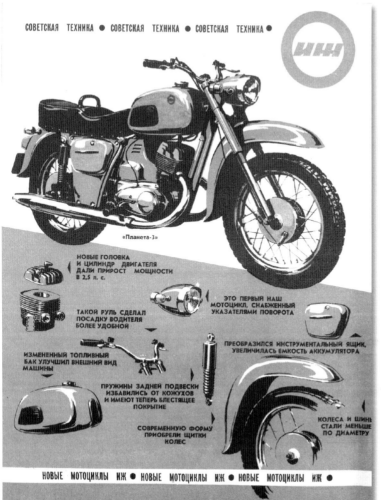

СОВЕТСКАЯ ТЕХНИКА ● СОВЕТСКАЯ ТЕХНИКА ● СОВЕТСКАЯ ТЕХНИКА ●

«Планета-3»

НОВЫЕ ГОЛОВКА
И ЦИЛИНДР ДВИГАТЕЛЯ
ДАЛИ ПРИРОСТ МОЩНОСТИ
В 2,5 л. с.

ЭТО ПЕРВЫЙ НАШ
МОТОЦИКЛ, СНАБЖЕННЫЙ
УКАЗАТЕЛЯМИ ПОВОРОТА

ТАКОЙ РУЛЬ СДЕЛАЛ
ПОСАДКУ ВОДИТЕЛЯ
БОЛЕЕ УДОБНОЙ

ИЗМЕНЕННЫЙ ТОПЛИВНЫЙ
БАК УЛУЧШИЛ ВНЕШНИЙ ВИД
МАШИНЫ

ПРЕОБРАЗИЛСЯ ИНСТРУМЕНТАЛЬНЫЙ ЯЩИК,
УВЕЛИЧИЛАСЬ ЕМКОСТЬ АККУМУЛЯТОРА

ПРУЖИНЫ ЗАДНЕЙ ПОДВЕСКИ
ИЗБАВИЛИСЬ ОТ КОЖУХОВ
И ИМЕЮТ ТЕПЕРЬ БЛЕСТЯЩЕЕ
ПОКРЫТИЕ

СОВРЕМЕННУЮ ФОРМУ
ПРИОБРЕЛИ ЩИТКИ
КОЛЕС

КОЛЕСА И ШИНЫ
СТАЛИ МЕНЬШЕ
ПО ДИАМЕТРУ

НОВЫЕ МОТОЦИКЛЫ ИЖ ● НОВЫЕ МОТОЦИКЛЫ ИЖ ● НОВЫЕ МОТОЦИКЛЫ ИЖ ●

IZH Planeta Sport, 1975. (Avtoexport)

made in the factory, it had little in common with the DKW heritage, and there were few common components. With help (it is said) from Yamaha, it initially boasted a Japanese Mikuni carburettor, Stanley electrics, and other modern fittings, including separate oil pump lubrication. The finish was in a striking yellow with a grey frame. Power was boosted to 30bhp giving it 140km/h potential. This is a bike that should have sold well abroad, and, with its modest price, won the USSR some much needed foreign currency (price in the UK in 1975 was £395, with a roughly equivalent Yamaha RD350cc costing

£479). However, the sales explosion did not happen: young western buyers still saw bikes from the USSR as utilitarian, cheap and inferior, and after the first few years the Japanese components were replaced with locally-made parts that reduced power. The model was dropped in 1983, the year which saw the introduction of the Planeta 4, another 350cc two-stroke with obvious lineage to the 45-year-old DKW. This again was twin port engined with 20bhp, and returned to a more conservative style – but with a nice red paint finish. This was superseded by the Planeta 5 in 1987, which saw some detail style changes to give it a look in keeping with the times, and a modest power increase. Sales of this model reached half a million, and they were popular, apparently, in China and some African countries.

Jupiter. 350cc's. 270£'s.

IZH Jupiter 3, 1975. (SATRA, UK importer)

The 350cc two-stroke twins

Intended originally to replace the postwar 350cc singles range, the Izhevsk-made 'Jupiter' series of 350cc two-stroke twins were introduced in 1961, after initial public exhibition display (at the Brussels World Fair) in 1957 as the IzH 58. These bikes were apparently developed in association with Jawa in Czechoslovakia, although the design differed significantly from the Jawa models that were very popular in the USSR. The new engine shared piston rods and bearings with the Kovrov 175cc single, but in an IZH 56 frame. Power was 18bhp, giving a top speed of 100km/h. Large numbers were sold fitted with matching sidecars.

The succeeding Jupiter 2, a similar bike with a slight power increase giving a higher top speed, was produced from 1965, before making way for the Jupiter 3 in 1970. The Jupiter 3 had the same styling modifications as the Planeta 3, but also a higher powered engine. This now provided up to 25bhp, giving a top speed of 120km/h. Production of the Jupiter 3 ended in 1980 to make way for the Jupiter 4, which again shared general styling and electrics improvements with its Planeta single stablemate. More power was extracted from engine and ignition modifications, so that bhp was now 28,

ИЖ·ЮПИТЕР·3K

IZH Jupiter 3K in a 'Beryozka' store leaflet, c1975. (Beryozka/Avtoexport)

IZH Jupiter 5, 1987. (Avtoexport)

IZH Jupiter 5 detail, 1986. (Avtoexport)

and top speed 125km/h. Like the other Soviet two-strokes of the 1980s, this was a good-looking bike whose cheap price ensured some export success. The Jupiter 5, followed in 1985, which also had some style updates. Although there was no great difference in performance, it did include a water-cooled variant. By this time, the powers that be had realised that two-strokes based on a prewar design were becoming very outdated, and plans were in hand to place a licensed copy of a Yamaha four-stroke 550cc single engine into the Izhevsk frame to create a new series of bike that could be turned out in various forms. However, there were numerous

GMZ M72 shown in *The Motor Cycle*, 10th February, 1949. (© Morton's Media)

B.M.W. 750 c.c. side-valve twin made in Russia and called the GMZ issues about such a technological leap: the supply of necessary components, suitable quality oil, and general cash shortage for the bike's development, and it was abandoned by 1988, the residual parts being used for continued Planeta and Jupiter production. Two-stroke production was eventually ended in the Izhevsk plant in post-USSR times, mainly due to growing emission controls in important export markets (Turkey and Iran banned two-strokes), but four-stroke replacements were only made for a few years before motorcycle production ended in 2008.

The 500cc, 650cc and 750cc flat-twin four-stroke motorcycles

The basic BMW lineage of the postwar M72 four-stroke flat-twin side-valve motorcycle (sometimes called a 'boxer' twin) was described in Chapter 1. The Soviet M72 developed during the war was a flat-twin side-valve four-stroke engine of 750cc capacity, giving 22bhp of power in an engine that could run quietly at very low rpm; this, and all subsequent models described below, were shaft driven. The plunger frame gave some spartan comfort to the rider.

Red Army postwar M72. (Author's collection)

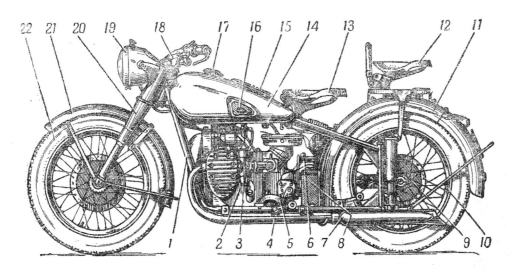

Рис. 1. Мотоцикл М-72 (общий вид):

1—рама; 2—двигатель; 3—карбюратор; 4—выпускная труба; 5—педаль ножного тормоза; 6—педаль пускового механизма; 7—глушитель; 8—аккумуляторная батарея; 9—телескопический кожух задней подвески; 10—заднее колесо; 11—задний щиток; 12—дополнительное седло; 13—седло водителя; 14—бензиновый бак; 15—инструментальный ящик; 16—резиновая подушка; 17—пробка бензинового бака; 18—руль; 19—фара; 20—передняя вилка; 21—передний щиток; 22—переднее колесо

M72 main components. (*Motorcycle Design*)

K750 main components. (*Heavy Motorcycles*)

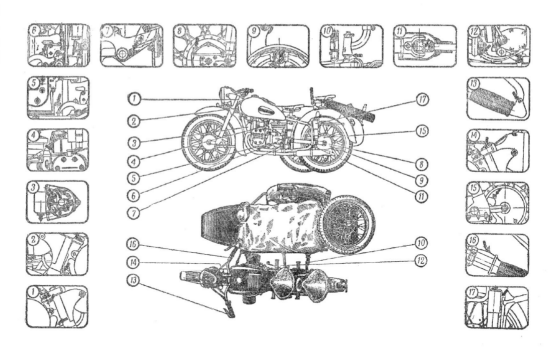

The well regarded K750 toolkit – typical of Soviet bikes. (Mukhin, P, Butenko, et al)

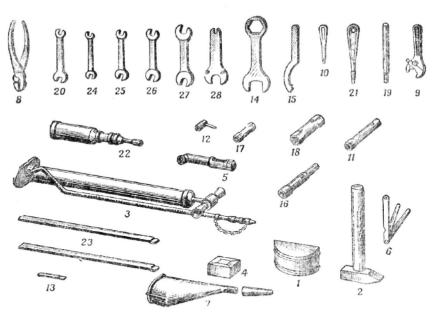

Рис. 88. Инструмент и принадлежности мотоцикла:

1 — автомотоаптечка; *2* — молоток; *3* — воздушный насос; *4* — аптечка генератора; *5* — манометр шинный; *6* — щуп в сборе; *7* — заправочная воронка с наконечником; *8* — плоскогубцы автомобильные; *9* — ключ гаечный разводной; *10* — отвертка малая; *11* — ключ торцовый 14 мм; *12* — ключ торцовый 8 мм; *13* — надфиль; *14* — ключ двухсторонний 36×41; *15* — ключ кольцевой; *16* — ключ торцовый 10×14; *17* — ключ торцовый 11×12; *18* — ключ торцовый 19×22; *19* — вороток; *20* — ключ гаечный 9×11; *21* — отвертка мотоциклетная; *22* — шприц штоковый; *23* — лопатка монтажная; *24* — ключ гаечный двухсторонний 8×10; *25* — ключ гаечный двухсторонний 12×14; *26* — ключ гаечный двухсторонний 14×17; *27* — ключ гаечный двухсторонний 19×22; *28* — ключ гаечный специальный двухсторонний

The sidecar versions were not driven (a proven off-road feature), but, as referred to in Chapter 1, a model known as the M73 was developed in 1943 that involved a sidecar drive mechanism and brake. However, as with other allied armies (eg the British Army with the Norton Big 4), it was dropped because of the widespread introduction of the US Willys Jeep. M72 production was initially just for military purposes, and it was not until the 1950s that civilian-intended manufacture commenced. The M72s produced in Moscow, Irbit, Gorky, and (later) Kiev, were almost identical, based as they were on the German BMW R71. There were differences: the petrol tank was larger at 22 litres, and there was other small detail variation. In 1944 the clutch was changed to twin plates, and other small chassis modifications made to improve strength to both bike and sidecar. Interestingly, during the war the technology seems to have been shared with the US military, as Harley Davidson created a side-valve flat-twin for army use (the XA), but, with the advent of the Jeep, it did not see volume production. At the war's end, the BMW plant captured by the Soviets was used as a source for developing production: manuals were copied, and BMW tooling purloined, some of which eventually finished up in the Nanchang Aircraft Manufacturing Corporation plant in China where the Chang Jiang is produced.

Whilst total M72 wartime output did not exceed 10,000 (there were far more US-made Harley Davidsons and Indians in Red Army service), postwar production was stepped up in both Irbit and Kiev, although exact numbers between the various plants does not seem to have been recorded anywhere. In Irbit the 30,000th M72 was produced in 1950 – the same figure being turned out annually following an upgrade to the plant in 1951. Civilian production began in Irbit in 1954, the year that exports, mostly for military uses, commenced to other countries. There were minor improvements in both factories reflecting the beginnings of diversity in development: in 1956 Irbit modified the brake hubs and strengthened the frame with the M72M, produced from then until the end of production the following year, when all the tooling was sold to China.

Meanwhile, the Kiev plant was also developing the model: the M72N appearing in the mid-1950s after the commencement of civilian production, with short leading link front forks. The Kiev plant gave the bike a more modern swinging arm frame, with the introduction of the K750 in 1959, also increasing engine power to 26bhp.

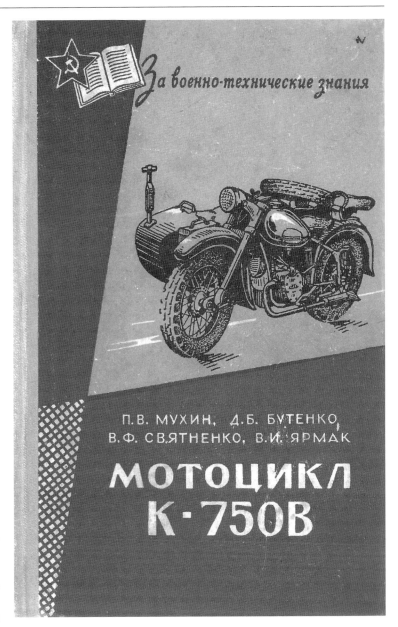

K750 manual cover. (Mukhin, P, Butenko et al)

The M72 continued in production (presumably to use up parts) for a few more years, but the K750, with refinements embodied in the K750M, became the standard side-valve model in the USSR until a major update with the Dnepr MT12 in 1977. The K750M also had a Kiev-made sidecar – previous ones being made in Irbit.

A 1964 variant for the military, the MV750 introduced a driven sidecar wheel with a differential lock for serious off road use, along with new and improved telescopic front forks. The MT12 replacement, a

M53 500cc, 1958.

(Avtoexport)

МОТОЦИКЛ М-53

Мотоцикл М-53 является машиной современной конструкции, предназначенной для езды в одиночку и с пассажиром в разнообразных дорожных условиях. Пригоден для туризма и деловых поездок, может быть использован с прицепной коляской.

Комфортабельность езды и надежность действия мотоцикла обеспечиваются благодаря применению карданной передачи, передней вилки рычажной системы и задней подвески рычажного типа.

Колеса снабжены мощными, независимо действующими тормозами, позволяющими быстро и плавно затормозить мотоцикл с самых больших скоростей движения. Оба колеса легкосъемной конструкции, взаимозаменяемы и имеют прямые спицы, что создает удобство при эксплуатации и надежность в работе.

Рама мотоцикла трубчатая, сварная, закрытого типа, обладает высокой прочностью при минимальном весе.

Топливный бак обтекаемой формы, красиво выгнутые выхлопные трубы и вытянутые большие глушители придают мотоциклу изящный вид.

Большое сдвоенное седло позволяет удобно разместиться водителю и пассажиру и улучшает внешний вид мотоцикла.

Мотоцикл окрашен в приятные тона, что в сочетании с многочисленными хромированными деталями придает машине нарядный внешний вид.

ТЕХНИЧЕСКАЯ ХАРАКТЕРИСТИКА

Общие данные. База — 1450 мм. Низшая точка — 160 мм. Вес мотоцикла (сухой) - 185 кг. Максимальная скорость — 125 км/час. Расход топлива на 100 км — 3,5 л. Емкость топливного бака —19 л. Расход масла — 0,15 л на 100 км. Емкость масляного резервуара — 2 л.

Двигатель — четырехтактный. Расположение клапанов — верхнее. Число цилиндров — 2. Рабочий объем цилиндров — 496 куб. см. Максимальная мощность — 28 л. с. при 5600 об/мин.

Система смазки — комбинированная.

Система питания — имеет два карбюратора, воздухоочиститель и топливный фильтр.

Зажигание — динамо-батарейное.

Освещение — фара, задний фонарь, стоп-сигнал.

Трансмиссия — Сцепление — сухое, двухдисковое. Коробка передач – двухходовая, четырехступенчатая. Переключение передач — ножное и ручное. Общие передаточные числа: 1-ая передача — 16,15, 2-ая передача — 10,55, 3-ья передача — 7,85 и 4-ая передача — 6,01.

Размер шин — 3,75 × 19".

MOTORCYCLE M-53

The M-53 motorcycle is of up-to-date design. It is intended for driving solo or with a passenger under diverse road conditions. It is suitable for touring and business journeys and can be used with a sidecar.

A lever type front fork, lever type rear suspension and propeller shaft transmission are used on the motorcycle to ensure high comfort and dependability.

The wheels are fitted with powerful independently acting brakes permitting rapid and smooth braking at the highest travelling speeds.

Both wheels are easily detachable, interchangeable and have straight spokes for convenience in service and reliability in operation.

The tubular welded closed type frame of the motorcycle is of minimum weight and yet extra strong.

The fuel tank is streamlined; the beautifully bent exhaust pipes and the elongated large silencers impart "streamlined beauty" to the M-53 motorcycle.

A large size double seat conveniently accommodates the driver and the passenger and improves the general appearance of the motorcycle.

The motorcycle is finished in pleasing tones, this in conjunction with the many chrome-plated parts imparts a handsome appearance to the machine.

SPECIFICATIONS

General data. Base — 1450 mm. Clearance — 160 mm. Weight of the motorcycle, dry — 185 kg. Maximum speed — 125 km/hr. Fuel consumption per 100 km — 3.5 l. Capacity of fuel tank — 19 l. Oil consumption per 100 km — 0.15 l. Oil system capacity — 2 l.

Engine. Four-stroke, 2-cylinder carburettor engine. Overhead valves. Displacement — 496 cu. cm. Maximum power — 28 h.p. at 5600 r.p.m.

Lubrication — combined type.

Fuel system. Comprises two carburettors, air cleaner and fuel filter.

Ignition system. Dynamo-battery.

Lighting. Headlamp, rear lamp and stop-light.

Clutch. Two-plate, dry type.

Transmission. Two-way, four-speed. The transmission gear case has manual and foot shifting. Gear ratios (total): first gear — 16.15, second gear — 10.55, third gear — 7.85 and fourth gear — 6.01.

Tyre size — 3.75 × 19".

simplified version of the MV750, was a beautiful bike, with plodding reliability, which shared cycle parts with the MT10 overhead valve described below, but with a longer frame. It had a reverse gear, automatic clutch and driven sidecar wheel as per the K750M, but lacked the differential lock which could be retro-fitted. This was the last side-valve motorcycle produced in the Soviet Union, lasting until 1985 (but, as previously noted, the M72 continues in China as the Chang Jiang M1, with an unsubstantiated rumour of a plant in North Korea that produced the same). Chief engineer at KMZ at the time of these developments, Pyotr Mukhin (principal author of the manual pictured on page 39) was allegedly sacked in 1974 for being late with the supply of escort motorcycles for senior government use.

The first overhead valve twin model, the M35 350cc, was made in the Gorky plant soon after the war as a racing model, but never went into volume production. Other 750cc overhead valve models for racing, the M75 series and the M76 and M77 were also developed through the course of the 1950s (described in Chapter 4). Production of a standard road model in Irbit came in 1956 with the 500cc M52, a model (along with its successor, the M53) which was made in small numbers, and is very rare today. A 650cc road model, the M61 followed in 1958, being superseded by the M62 in 1960, a model with some improvements, but, as with all the models mentioned in this paragraph, using the M72 plunger chassis and cycle parts.

The M61 and other overhead valve variants owed their origins to BMW designs that were studied by Soviet technicians and designers at the war's end. It is interesting to note that these 650cc OHV models used the 78mm bore from the R71/M72 and the 68mm stroke from the BMW 500cc engines, resulting in 649cc – a very non-BMW capacity. The M62 in 1960 became the first mass-produced overhead valve model, and also the first to be given the 'Ural' brand name which has been used ever since.

The Soviet OHV 650cc bikes differed greatly from the heavyweight BMW R75 and Zundapp K750 sidecar-driving machines in widespread use by the German Army during the war. Many of these were captured during the conflict and were in Red Army use for many years afterwards. They had great off-road capability, and there is speculation that their presence in large numbers prevented the Soviets from developing their own motorcycle with driven sidecar wheel until the 1960s.

Significant improvement to the 650cc overhead valve models came with the Ural

M62 650cc, 1960.
(Avtoexport)

M63 650cc, c1967. (Avtoexport)

M66 650cc, 1972. (Avtoexport)

41

**K650, c1972.
(Avtoexport)**

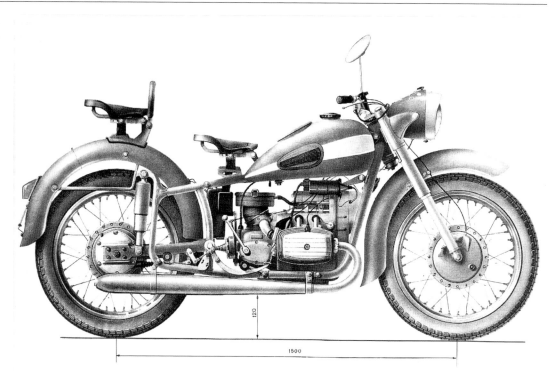

M63 model from Irbit in 1965: a swinging arm frame, and style similar to those still in production. The Ural M66 in 1968 brought in the shape of petrol tank that was to remain with all the successor models, and a slight increase in engine power to 30bhp, giving a top speed for a solo machine of 105km/h. Meanwhile, similar developments were under way in Kiev: the 'Dnepr' K650 overhead valve twin was introduced in 1967, ostensibly to celebrate the October revolution of 1917. There were significant differences between these and the Irbit-produced models: the Ural

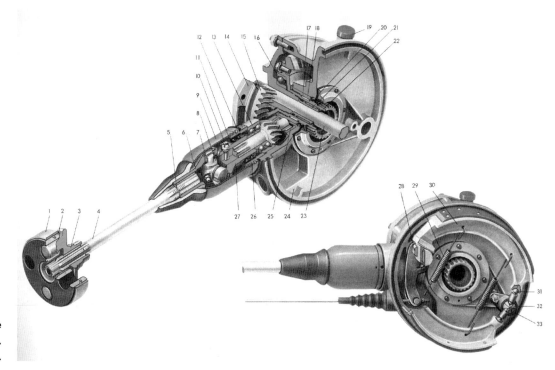

**K650 rear drive
detail, 1972.
(Avtoexport).**

engine had a pressed up crank with roller bearings, and iron cylinder barrels, but the Dnepr engine had a one piece crank, shell big-ends, and aluminium barrels with steel liners. The Ural frame had a swinging arm outside of the rear frame tubes, and bonded rubber bushes, whilst the Dnepr frame had a swinging arm inside the rear frame tubes, and loose rubber bushes; the Dnepr frame was also longer than the Ural frame. The K650 engine had more power than its predecessor at 32bhp. The 'Dnepr' name was to be given to all the subsequent models from Kiev. The K650 was renamed the Dnepr MT8 around 1969, and then replaced by the MT9, which had 34bhp and a better front brake, in 1971. The MB650 variant for the Red Army had a driven sidecar wheel and a differential lock (as with the side-valve military bikes) not available on the civilian models. The final MT9 models were given the new tank design that became a distinctive feature of all the subsequent Dnepr models. This more modern look was incorporated into the MT10 in 1973, which also had 12-volt electrics. An 'update' of this model, the MT10-36 of 1976, brought in engine improvements, and a power increase to 36bhp that saw it achieve 110km/h in solo form, but with the older style swinging arm frame. One of these became the millionth motorcycle produced in Kiev in 1979.

Over at the Irbit plant, the M67 650cc overhead valve of 1973 had increased engine power to 32bhp, 12-volt electrics and a new and longer swinging arm frame. Power was increased again to 36bhp with the M67-36, in 1976. These had a reputation as unreliable models, but were produced in very large numbers for civilian use, and became common sights throughout the Soviet Union and the countries to whom they were exported – especially those where such machines were for workhorse rather than leisure use. The final overhead valve twins of the Soviet era from Dnepr were the MT11, which had an improved tappet design over the MT10-36, and the MT16 model that was introduced in 1981, both of which had the same sidecar drive as the MT12 side-valve bikes. These models formed the basis

Dnepr MT9, 1972. (Avtoexport)

of production in various guises and style forms, until the closure of the factory in post-Soviet times, and one became the two millionth motorcycle produced at Kiev in 1989. The factory also produced variants of its products for cheap commercial use, such as a fire-fighting sidecar combination, but these were not successes. KMZ also collaborated with Neval in the UK (see Chapter 3) to develop machines aimed at export markets, the 1990 'Roadster' and 'Classic' models being examples.

In Irbit the final USSR-produced models were the IMZ 8.103 family, produced in various forms from 1983, including latterly

Table medal commemorating the one millionth motorcycle produced in Kiev, 1979. (Author's collection)

Table medal commemorating the two millionth motorcycle produced in Kiev, 1989. (Author's collection)

the 'Tourist' model. These machines had an increase in power to 32bhp in sidecar hauling form, and 36bhp in solo form. No further power increases followed, as a decision was made to focus on use with low quality fuels. Like their Dnepr counterparts, options were available including leading link front forks (designs differed between the IMZ and KMZ factories), reverse gear, and sidecar drive. By this time production in Irbit was aimed at Western enthusiast markets, and specifications reflect that. The scaled down factory continues to make direct and very similar descendants of these models – their high price and

Enot M 'Raccoon' trailer. (Vostok Motorcycles)

relative rarity being directed at a leisure market, especially in destinations such as the USA – a long way from the workaday use of those produced in Soviet times!

SIDECARS AND TRAILERS

Sidecars were always a feature of production and sales of the heavyweight motorcycles. Indeed, in the Soviet period, it would be unusual to see a solo motorcycle from the Irbit or Kiev factories. They were used for the transport of people and goods for work and leisure purposes, as can be seen from the images throughout this book (especially in Chapter 5). This continued throughout the Soviet period as cars remained out of reach for most citizens. These were produced in the same factories that made the motorcycles. Some sidecars, and not just those in military use, were driven – a useful feature in the countryside where roads were (and still often are) unmade and rough.

Sidecars were also a distinctive feature of both single and twin 350cc Izhevsk motorcycles, and were made from 1956 for the factory in the Vyatskiye-Polyany (VMPZ) plant, which more famously produced scooters. These of course made for cheap family transport before cars became available at an affordable price towards the end of the Soviet era.

They were also fitted to the twins exported abroad – including the UK – but by the time they started arriving, the days of popular sidecar use were over for ever with the advent of the Mini and other budget cars.

Trailers were an obvious addition to motorcycles – whether or not with sidecars, for the carriage of additional luggage. From the 1980s these were produced under the *Enot* brand name in volume specifically for the cheap 175cc Voskhod motorcycle range – initially by the PAZ Bus Plant, and then in the Kovrov factory itself. They were known as 'Raccoons,' were small in size and could carry up to about 80kg – a little more than their own weight. They were fitted with lighting for use in urban areas.

3 EXPORTS & EVALUATIONS: THE VIEW FROM THE UK

INTRODUCTION

Exports were never a significant component of the Soviet economy, based as it was on ideological notions of self-sufficiency and a reality that took account of the country's vast natural resources. In 1985, for example, foreign trade represented 4% of Soviet GDP: a significantly lower figure than that of western countries. However, the earning of hard foreign currency became a concern as the economy began to stagnate in the 1970s, and exports of manufactured goods (along with oil and gas) became of increasing importance, so that the country could, for example, import grain to feed its people. Most Soviet-built motorcycles were exported to friendly countries within the 'Soviet Bloc,' and for that reason are still to be found in numbers in places such as Cuba, Vietnam,

Afghanistan, Egypt, parts of Africa, and, of course, Eastern Europe.

This chapter looks at Soviet motorcycle exports generally, and particularly through the prism of the British experience. It takes the opportunity to assess how Soviet-built machines were experienced through the commentaries available in the contemporary motorcycle press of the day. Such tests are of value when looking at performance and quality, according to the standards of the times in which they were written. Some were flavoured by anti-USSR prejudice, but most were objective and fair – even if they did at times annoy importers.

AVTOEXPORT

When exports of manufactured goods began to be taken seriously within the

Avtoexport Head Office, Moscow. (Avtoexport)

Zapchastexport English language parts list for Voskhod 2, c1973.
(Zapchastexport)

USSR's economy in the late 1950s, the Soviet Government established a central agency with the specific task of promoting and arranging the export of cars, commercial vehicles, motorcycles and bicycles: 'Avtoexport' had its central offices in a large building in Moscow, and, over the years, turned out regular promotional material in foreign languages, including English. Avtoexport was also responsible for imports: this was consistent with the planned aspect of the Soviet economy, where considerations other than market-driven demand predominated – examples will be given in Chapter 5. Alongside Avtoexport, another agency was similarly responsible for international spares distribution: 'Zapchastexport.'

One of the first international events of importance to Avtoexport was the International World Fair in Brussels in 1958. The USSR had a large, impressive and award-winning pavilion at the Fair, in which it showcased its technical achievements, including the Sputnik satellite (a model of which mysteriously disappeared!), the nuclear powered icebreaker *Lenin*, cars, lorries and motorcycles. This was followed by an appearance of motorcycles at the Leipzig Trade Fair in 1960, with glossy foreign language brochures explaining the technical details of the M103, the K175, the Planeta, the Jupiter, the M62, the K750, and various scooter models. By 1970, Avtoexport was trading with 75 countries in a range of manufactured automotive industry products.

Foreign customers could also order a motorcycle individually through 'Vneshposyltorg' (All-Union Foreign Mail Order Trade Association), a state organisation in the Soviet Union selling goods for foreign currency – in effect, a mail order company. This organisation, from 1964 (after economic reforms), provided 'Beryozka' stores in the USSR, which only sold 'luxury goods' that might be hard to buy anywhere else – a strange phenomenon that allowed some Soviet citizens to buy export goods at home that were never intended for export. Soviet citizens who received an income in foreign currency were made to change it into

'Vneshposyltorg cheques' which were in USSR roubles, and could be exchanged in these stores. Cheques were a form of soviet currency of limited usage, available only for those who were working abroad in the present or recent past. Usually 60% of a salary abroad was transferred to the earner's bank account in the USSR, and became available upon their return. Another 40% was paid abroad in local currency to support living whilst there. A limited time after the end of foreign contact, these cheques had to be spent (in Beryozka stores or as a deposit for an apartment), or the Soviet citizen concerned could be prosecuted for keeping illegal currency. These stores sold motorcycles for foreign currency to foreign visitors, and to Soviet citizens as described.

EXPORTS TO BRITAIN

According to the Cossack Owners' Club (whose website notes have been sourced for this section), exports to Britain had taken place prior to 1970 in very small numbers. Certainly, a feature in the September 1970 issue of *Motorcycle Sport* (*MCS*) about some models that turned up in Canada, was unaware of their presence in the United Kingdom. However, by mid-1971, imports to the UK of the M63 650cc Ural seem to have been well established through a concession handled by Fred Wells, from his motorcycle shop in London. He, in turn, distributed them to a number of other dealers in the London area. All this was reported in *MCS* for June 1971, in which Mr Wells claimed to have over 300 orders. Fred Wells produced instruction booklets in English, and promoted the model by riding one across the Sahara. However, in 1973, a more elaborate concession was established by the New York based SATRA (Soviet American Trade), which increased promotional efforts of a wider range until 1979. In addition to the flat-twin overhead-valve models, the Riga 50cc moped, Minsk 125cc, Voskhod 175cc, Planeta 340cc and 350cc, and Jupiter 350cc models were offered. SATRA also, and primarily, imported cars and Belarus-built tractors (becoming known as SATRA Belarus), being based initially

Avtoexport multi-language brochure for 1960 Leipzig Trade Fair. (Avtoexport)

MOTORCYCLE "VOSKHOD"

The "Voskhod" motorcycle is a small-capacity roadster capable of carrying a rider and a pillion passenger.

This exceptionally handy machine is fitted with an engine powerful enough to drive it under various road conditions.

Riding comfort is catered for by the provision of a telescopic front fork and a swinging rear fork controlled by hydraulic dampers.

Deep mudguards effectively protect the driver and the machine against dirt.

Driving safety is assured by a hand brake on the front wheel and a foot brake on the rear wheel.

The machine is finished in pleasing colour schemes. Chrome plating on the handlebar, silencer, control lever and other small parts add to the smartness of the appearance.

SPECIFICATIONS

Wheelbase, *mm* . . . . not more	1300
Ground clearance under silencer, fully laden, *mm* . . . . not less	100
Dry weight, *kg* . . . . not more	110
Maximum speed on highway, *km/hr* . . . . not less	90
Fuel consumption per 100 *km, l* . . . . not more	2.8
Fuel tank capacity, *l*	13
Engine . . . . two-cycle, petrol, carburettor	
Power output after running-in, *hp* . . . . not less	10
Displacement, *cu.cm* 173.7	
Cooling . . . . by air	
Fuel . . . . 20:1 petrol/oil mixture during running-in period;	
	25:1 petrol/oil mixture after running-in

Vneshposyltorg leaflet for Voshkod 175, c1962. (Vneshposyltorg)

Beryozka leaflet for IZH Jupiter 3K, c1978. (Beryozka)

ТЕХНИЧЕСКАЯ ХАРАКТЕРИСТИКА

```
База, мм .......................................... 1450
Дорожный просвет, мм ........................ 115
Габариты, мм ..................... 2200×1600×1300
Сухой вес, кг ..................................... 253
Максимальная скорость, км/ч ............... 90
Тормозной путь при движении со скоростью
30 км/ч .............................................. 7,2
Расход топлива при движении со ско-
ростью 50—60 км/ч на горизонтальном
асфальтированном шоссе, л/100 км ...... 5,8
Средний эксплуатационный расход
топлива при движении в различных
дорожных условиях л/100 км ........... 7,0—8,0
Емкость топливного бака, л ................... 18
Топливо ................................... бензин А-72
Двигатель ......... двухтактный, двухцилиндровый
Рабочий объем, см³ ............................. 347
Степень сжатия ............................... 8,5—9
Максимальная мощность, л.с. ............... 25
Система смазки .................. совместно с топливом
Система зажигания ..................... батарейная
Воздухоочиститель .............. контактно-масляный
Охлаждение ................................... воздушное
Сцепление ......... многодисковое в масляной ванне
Коробка передач ................... четырехступенчатая
Колеса ........................... взаимозаменяемые
Размер шин ...................... 90-459 (3,5-18)
```

Цена: 1040 руб. в сертификатах В/О „Внешпосы-
торг" с отличительной синей полосой.

СССР, 121200 Москва Г-200
Смоленская-Сенная пл., 32/34
В/О „Внешпосылторг"
Телекс: 7250
Телефон: 241-89-39

ИЖ-ЮПИТЕР-3К

Дорожный мотоцикл „Иж-Юпитер-3К" хорош
для деловых и туристических поездок.
Двигатель и силовая передача мотоцикла
надежны и долговечны. Механизм автомати-
ческого выжима сцепления облегчает управ-
ление, а подвески колес обеспечивают высокую плавность хода. Цепная передача на
заднее колесо герметически закрыта.
„ИЖ-Юпитер-3К" снабжен комфорта-
бельной коляской, имеющей сдвижной капот
с ветровым стеклом, съемное сиденье и
спинку, а в передней части перекидной упор
для ног. Колесо коляски снабжено тормо-
зом, действующим от рычага ножного тормоза мотоцикла, и маятниковой подвеской с
гидравлическим амортизатором, унифициро-
ванным с амортизаторами подвески заднего
колеса мотоцикла.
Современные обтекаемые формы мотоцикла и коляски, двухцветная окраска,
хромированные детали придают мотоциклу
привлекательный вид.

В/О "ВНЕШПОСЫЛТОРГ"

in the UK in Surrey, and then, from 1975, in Carnaby near Bridlington in Yorkshire. SATRA registered 'Cossack' as a brand for all the Soviet-built motorcycles, a name still associated with Russian motorcycles of that era and beyond. The SATRA set-up involved major investment with plush offices, expensive promotional effort, and huge display stands at the London Motorcycle Shows. Sales of motorcycles however, despite at one point having 210 dealers throughout the UK, were not good. Contemporary tests will be considered below, but it is worth at this point passing on the impressions of marque expert Peter Ballard who was a fitter/tester for SATRA towards the end of its concession period:

"The motorcycles, sadly, got a poor reputation: they were being presented as modern motorcycles, but they were not. Most had poor brakes and would suffer from high speed use in Europe. The 'Retro' angle was never exploited. I always got the impression that although the bikes SATRA sold were export specification with chrome rims etc, they were often not the latest models … Many of the bikes had damage to them due to the shipping from the USSR, and standing around in crates outside for up to three years … Chrome work was often pitted and needed replacement; engines, gearboxes and final drives had water in them, paintwork often needed resprays … I think that, considering the quality of the bikes they bought, they (SATRA) did really well to put out well prepared bikes with a really professional approach. Sadly the purchasers of the bikes often neglected them, resulting in poor reliability."
(Reproduced with permission from the Cossack Owners' Club Website)

Just who exactly was the Cossack poster advert with the 'leggy' model aimed at? (See colour gallery, page 72.) Given that most of those imported were attached to sidecars, it seems unlikely that they would appeal to potential customers who were wooed by similar contemporary advertisements for the latest Japanese multi-cylinder superbikes.

The New Cossack Minsk.125cc.

The ideal small bike for the commuter or the young sportsman, the Cossack 125cc Minsk offers lightness, reliability and a most economical ride at its size. Indeed, pricewise, it can match machines with half its capacity and zest.

It is a bike with a breezy and pleasant nature, with a mirror, and the usual comprehensive Cossack toolkit.

Styled for pleasure, built for reliability, and priced for economy, the Cossack Minsk 125 is the perfect bike for getting into or out of town, going to the shops—or for the young enthusiast to show his paces.

The Minsk 125cc is the kind of bike that a fond father would consider as a reward for his off-spring's good exam results. And then buy for himself.

Specification:

Engine. Single Cylinder, 2-Stroke	Primary Drive. Single Row Chain in Oil Bath
Bore. 52mm	Gear Ratios. 1st 21·796–1, 2nd 17·735–1, 3rd 9·773–1, 4th 7·372–1
Stroke. 58mm	
Capacity. 125cc	Tyres. 2.50 x 19"
BHP. 9.5 at 6,000rpm	Frame. Tubular Welded
Fuel Grade. Petroil 25 to 1	Front Fork. Telescopic
Air Cleaner. Contact Oil Type	Tank. 2·5 gallons
Clutch. Multi-Disc in Oil Bath	Weight. 224lbs.

SATRA Cossack UK leaflet for the Minsk 125cc, 1975. (SATRA/ Avtoexport)

Nev Mason (see his autobiography *100%*), who began very successful marketing of the Minsk 125cc models from his Hull dealership in the mid-1970s, was quick to point out the sales weakness to the Soviets, and eventually secured the concession for the motorcycles (SATRA continued to deal in car and other vehicle imports), along with his partner Alan Voase in 1979. Their first names were combined to create the 'Neval' brand name, used until after the end of the Soviet era (and Nev Mason's departure from the firm in the mid-1980s). Mason and Voase maintained a strict pre-delivery inspection (PDI) regime from the outset of their involvement with SATRA, and made modifications to the bikes, such as longer brake arms which improved brake efficiency, and a better rear lamp.

The Neval concession from 1979 adopted an aggressive and very profitable approach to marketing, targeting different audiences for the MMZ, KMZ and IMZ models it imported – the Minsk 125cc models were cheap, no frills, get to work bikes, just as small British two-strokes had been a decade or two earlier, and were advertised as such in the national tabloids, rather than the motorcycle press. The Dnepr models were contrastingly aimed at motorcycle enthusiasts looking for retro style. Neval also kept overheads to a minimum, and put aside the expensive promotional efforts of SATRA. Over time, Neval also influenced export development and quality issues at the Kiev and Minsk factory end, and secured improvements and modifications that aided its sales efforts in Europe and North America. These included the fitment of different carburettors, left hand dipping headlights, electronic ignition, tyres, brakes, custom styling additions and also engine work (eg, end float shimming on the Dnepr 650 bikes). In his memoir, Nev Mason states that in Kiev he got agreement that all components would be of the 'Red Star' quality demanded by the Soviet military. Whatever he was told, this is very unlikely to have been a reality: the Red Star mark (or other mark accepted by the military, as some were hidden) was only applied to components supplied to the military, and was in effect a certification that the item had been inspected by a Defence Ministry representative, as well as a factory technician; this would not have been undertaken for any other customer.

Classic Styling and simple robust reliability makes this motorcycle as individual and admired as high-tech sophisticated machines. Without costing the earth, a lifetime investment you will be proud to own.

Brief specification
Engine: Horizontally opposed twin cylinder OHV 4 stroke air cooled.
Capacity: 649cc. 8.5:1 compression ratio
Bore×Stroke: 78×68mm.
Brakes: Drum. Front twin leading shoe.
Maindrive: Shaft to Crown wheel & pinion.
Ignition and Lights: 12 volt Auto advance.
Alternator: 150W/12 Volt.

Tyres: 4.10×19 Avon Roadrunner.
Clutch: dry twin disc.
Gearbox: 4 speed with reverse.
Carburettor: twin K62 28mm.
Suspension: Rear adjustable hydraulic shock absorber
Front Hydraulic telescopic fork
Dry Weight: 245 Kg

Equipment
Single saddles or dual seat. Mirror. Sidestand and mainstaind. 34 piece tool and spares kit. Indicators.

Optional Equipment
Rear carrier, full fairing, electronic ignition, crashbars, legshields.

Specifications may be subject to alteration

NEVAL MOTORCYCLES LTD.
''Brockholme'', Seaton Road, Hornsea, HU18 1BZ
Telephone: 0964 533878

Designed, photographed and printed by Just Leaflets & Catalogues Ltd. 142 Merton Hall Road, Wimbledon Chase, London, SW19 3PZ, Tel: 01-543 3855/6/7/8/9

Neval Cossack leaflet for Dnepr Classic 650, c1990. (Neval Motorcycles, UK)

USSR factory visits attracted the attention, so Nev Mason states, of the British Secret Service, MI5, who invited him to spy for them, an offer apparently declined. By the early 1980s, Nev Mason quotes import figures of 250 Dnepr outfits, 50 Dnepr solos and 750 Minsk 125s a year, and claims that there were few warranty issues due to the company's customer-friendly practices and strict PDIs. In the 1980s, Neval also imported some of the later IZH Planeta 5 and Jupiter 5 models, but they were never sold in great numbers. By the end of the Soviet era in 1990-1991, models such as the Dnepr 'Classic' and 'Roadster' 650 flat-twins bore little resemblance to anything for the home market in the USSR, being custom finished in the UK with parts

obtained elsewhere. A later post-Soviet development involved a BMW R80 engine in a Dnepr frame. The franchise for the larger post-Soviet machines still under production in Irbit eventually passed to UralMoto UK, with the market in cheap 'ride to work' bikes being later cornered by Chinese manufacturers.

THE BRITISH PRESS

An early mention of Soviet motorcycles in the postwar British motorcycling press was in the 'Four Winds' column, by 'Nitor,' in *The Motor Cycle* of 10 February 1949: photographs and an accompanying, but brief, account is given of the Moskva 125, the IZH 350 and a Gorky-manufactured M72 (not identified as such). It is clear that the author had little information, beyond opinion, that each of these models had German origins, and he ends by appealing for more from readers. Fast forward to 1961, and the 13th July issue of *Motor Cycling* had some coverage of Soviet motorcycles shown at a large Soviet Trade Exhibition in Earls Court, London that year. Some detailed commentary of the four machines on display, based on visual examination, is made by leading motorcycle engineer and designer Phil Irving. He notes that, technically, the road bikes (a 650cc, wrongly described by Irving as 600cc, Ural overhead-valve with sidecar, a Jupiter twin and a Kovrovets 175cc) offered no innovations, and were of rugged design but well coated in chrome and satin-finished aluminium castings. He comments on the "modern styling" and attractive blue finish of the two-strokes, and their resemblance to Jawa machines; contrastingly, he regards the Ural as "grim and forbidding in appearance," but notes the robust sidecar design with the three wheels of the combination being interchangeable. He was more taken with the fourth bike on show, a 250cc C259 race bike, of which more in Chapter 4. The article also noted that although there were no prices displayed, the expectation seemed to be that these bikes were to be exported to the UK by Avtoexport, which wanted to break into the British market. This show report was accompanied by an insightful first hand report from the USSR with a commentary on the state of motorcycling and the motorcycle industry. This pointed to the popularity of motorcycles, with their appeal being bolstered by the out-of-reach nature of car ownership – not that different from home in those days!

These impressions from visual inspection were to be overtaken by regular road tests and reviews, once import to the UK began in earnest in the 1970s. An early one, based on actual and detailed testing of an M63 650cc solo, appeared in *MCS* in June 1971. Much of the article is taken up with just how much is copied from old BMW designs, a case being made for gross plagiarism. However, the piece justifies this by looking at the purpose and functionality of the machine, excusing its "ugliness" on the same grounds. The brakes are heavily criticised, as are the sidecar gearing, 6-volt electrics, hard suspension, gear change lever, engine oil leaks and overall finish quality. However, the tester concluded that the Ural provided a "smooth and pleasant" ride, and forgave its inadequacies by reference to its very cheap purchase price (less than half the cost of any other similar capacity machine), pointing out that it offered good value for money.

The Voskhod 175, which first appeared in 1973, was tested by *MCS* in December 1974 and found wanting in several areas – but not the brakes, the front one had by then been modified for the UK market. The major criticisms were of mechanics, the finish, and Russian-made tyres that affected handling. Fuel economy was good, as was comfort, and, of course, the remarkably low price received favourable comment. This report was put into perspective through a follow-up article in *MCS* of February 1975, by Thomas Mahoney of Perthshire who had put 30,000 miles onto his Voskhod, and had nothing but praise for its simplicity. He had purchased the bike for a daily 30-mile journey to work, in all seasons and weathers, and found it to be exactly what he needed, with the weather protective legshields and windscreen very good. Mr Mahoney even used his bike for two up touring, and found it up to the task. He had some issues with

> IT is excusable to glance at the Russian machines shown on these pages and pronounce them German. Essentially they *are* German, but produced in Russia. The Moskva is a 125 c.c. two-stroke, or a former **RUSSIAN MACHINES** D.K.W. with a Russian name; it may be had in various attractive pastel finishes. Larger two-stroke is the Izh 350, a direct copy of the D.K.W. NZ1 *circa* 1943, a 350 c.c. single with nothing especially outstanding about it. This model is, I gather, a popular mount for Soviet cross-country trials of the long-distance type which are steadily gaining popularity. Finally the sidecar outfit is the GMZ (probably means Gorky Motorcycle Works) and is the B.M.W. 750 c.c. side-valve model R71 which was, in fact, made under licence in the Soviet Union in 1939; it was then called the M71. A significant point about nearly all Soviet motor cycles of which details have come my way is that they are a crib from Germany. With cars, the crib is usually from American designs. I have occasionally seen photographs of "unknown" machines but have never obtained technical details; in one instance the "new model" was obviously a mock up which, to my understanding, could not possibly have worked. If we have any Russian readers, could they supply me with details of any home-designed and built Russian motor cycles?

'Nitor' feature in *The Motor Cycle*, 10 February, 1949. (© Mortons Media)

the electrics, and dumped the indicators early on. The fairness of this report was in its comparison with similarly basic British bikes that by then were no longer available, but missed by riders like him.

A detailed test of a new Ural 650cc, this time a sidecar combination, was offered in *Motorcycle Mechanics* in February 1975. Brakes had been improved with linings specially fitted for the export market, but most of the criticisms of the model were listed again. However, economy was restated as an overwhelming positive, and the comprehensive tool kit particularly praised. *MCS* of March 1975 had a test of a 650cc combination, and again complained of poor brakes, lighting and finish quality, with a detailed description of the "agricultural" and "crude" feel to the bike. Again, however, the cheap price and potential reliability were considered virtues, and enjoyment would follow so long as the potential owner understood the drawbacks of the machine. The same issue contained a less than flattering test account of the Jupiter 350cc two-stroke twin. This noted its ugly appearance and poor finish, alongside technical defects such as very poor braking, inadequate clutch control, and poor fuel economy. On the plus side, performance and comfort (after modification) were good, as was ease of maintenance. Included was a common observation with these tests, the notion that at half the price of equivalent sized machines, you get what you pay for – but even at that, the generally liked, but also basic, Jawa 350cc from Czechoslovakia was at that time still cheaper. The tester had the bike for three weeks, and felt that, even if used as transport only, it missed out entirely on the "fun" essence of motorcycling.

A Minsk 125 bike supplied by Neval was tested by *Bike* magazine in May 1977, alongside nine other similar capacity machines from across the world. The report was scathing of the Minsk, criticising almost every aspect of the bike and not excusing it on price grounds (it was considerably cheaper than all the others, including the MZ and CZ machines from Eastern Europe). Starting out with a swipe at the whole Soviet bike industry the review went on to describe the machine as "… one of the most objectionable examples of almost Neanderthal motorcycle engineering available in Britain," and photographed it on a pile of rubbish! *Bike* had condemned a SATRA-supplied Voskhod 175cc some years earlier as the worst bike it had ever seen, but this report went even further. The brakes and lights on the Minsk were said to be so poor as to be dangerous, and potential purchase "… a two-wheeled version of Russian roulette." Nev Mason of Neval was so annoyed by the review that he refused to supply a test bike to *Bike* four years later, and a thaw only set in after his departure from the company. However, improvements were made, and quickly (a total of 22 improvements were advertised, including 6-volt electronic ignition), because a comprehensive *Which Bike* assessment in May 1978, set against a Suzuki A100, put it ahead on a number of points – including price. This test pointed out that the cheapness of imported Soviet machines was offset by expensive part replacement, but that seemed to have been rectified with the Minsk (at least).

MCS, in October 1980, contained an account of nine years and 26,000 miles of UK ownership of a 650cc Ural machine, from which the sidecar was removed after about 12,000 miles. This test makes technical comparisons with British bikes rather than, as found in the tests already quoted, with flat-twin BMW models. The owner made practical modifications over the years, usefully listed in the article along with the modest cost of all additional expenditure, and was pleased with his machine as a country lane and town riding bike.

In April 1983, the magazine *Mechanics and the Biker* tested a Dnepr 650 MT10 with sidecar. This bike carried a purchase price of £1459, and was therefore not considered cheap (the same issue reviewed a sophisticated Kawasaki Z750 priced at £1899, and advertised the Neval Minsk 125cc at a bargain £345). Unlike its predecessors, featured in the reviews already quoted, this bike had all the Neval modifications: SU carburettor, Bosch contact breakers, Nippo Denso coil, Japanese 12-volt battery, tachometer, Avon tyres on Spanish alloy rims, twin leading shoe front brake with improved cable, and better quality internal engine parts. However, there were still criticisms of braking quality and control components – both electrical and mechanical. Overall, the tester was impressed with comfort and performance, but underwhelmed by the "rugged simplicity" of the bike.

By the 1980s, of course, sidecar machines were an anachronistic rarity on UK roads, and only used by enthusiasts

Minsk 125. (*Bike* magazine, May 1977)

Dnepr 650 (far left) with Eastern European bikes. (© *Superbike* magazine, May 1988)

– those seeking family transport had long ago stepped up to car ownership (or with their full motorcycle licences, to the three-wheeled Reliant Robin). The fact that they were still used for everyday use on the other side of the Iron Curtain exercised its own fascination with motorcycle journalists, resulting in some rather tongue-in-cheek testing. One such example was in *SuperBike* magazine for May 1988, which featured a test of a Neval Dnepr MT11 combination alongside Eastern European solos from MZ and Jawa, under the title "Socialist Weaklies." By this time, the Neval operation, although importing a claimed 250 machines a year, had scaled back to sole UK dealership and (by now very efficient) parts supply. The test itself was quite superficial, and full of stereotypical references to the USSR intended to raise a laugh amongst the readership, its authors being more usually concerned with the latest large capacity superbikes. It did raise some serious points relating to quality and braking – much as previously reported elsewhere – but felt the bike was cheap (the price had hardly risen since 1983, despite rapid inflation affecting other bike prices), and therefore worth consideration.

A similarly fun-poking test appeared in *Bike* magazine in August 1985 – this time of a Ural 650cc solo ex-showroom demonstration bike, supplied at short notice through Neval. It was accompanied by photographs of tester, Roland Brown, wearing a Red Army greatcoat and 'ushanka' fur-lined hat, with a Kalashnikov sub-machine gun strapped to his shoulder. On the serious side, it again criticised brake performance and irritations such as a leaking petrol tap, but praised improvements to switchgear and the 12-volt electrics. It noted that with quality improvements now being made at the factory end, Neval had to make few modifications itself. The tester liked the bike for its idiosyncrasies and antique manners, but still had to admit, objectively, that it was "an awful motorcycle."

The final motorcycle press article in

The Ural 650, made fun of by Roland Brown in *Bike* magazine. (© Tony Sleep, 1985)

this review appeared in *Used Bike Guide* in August 1989, based on one owner's experience since purchase of a Ural 650cc some two years earlier, and another similar bike purchased secondhand. This was generally favourable, and correctly placed the bikes in their true context – neither comparing them with BMWs or contemporary superbikes. Simplicity and ease of maintenance are praised, although – as with every test – standard fittings like carburettors and electrical switches criticised.

Poor braking seems to be a recurrent theme of tests (but not all) throughout the late Soviet period. Nev Mason suggested that the Minsk 125 was deliberately supplied with a poor front brake to make for safer stopping in the Russian snow. This might have been sales-spin of course, and he did make every effort to deal with the issue for UK roads. This trait had a strange outcome for the Voskhod

2 175cc shown at the Stafford Classic Bike Show in April 2018 (see page 73, top picture): John Chrystal's bike had been abandoned by its owner, and consigned to a shed soon after purchase in 1977 from a Manchester dealer, due, it was said, to death-trap braking. Although the chrome had entirely peeled off over the years, and had been replaced at no little expense, the smart orange paintwork was as-new, and the clock mileage a genuine 35km.

So the British motorcycle press of the 1970s and 1980s never really took to motorcycles made in the USSR – regarding them as generally cheap and inferior, and contributing to a generally held public view that itself reflected the West versus East climate of the cold war. Of course it might have been different had they been imported in numbers in the 1950s, when the average British motorcyclist was riding similar machines, of similar quality, of mostly home manufacture, and for mostly the same reasons as USSR users. The low price of the Urals, Dneprs and their smaller Soviet cousins, their home maintenance friendly, rugged style, and construction, might have been regarded a lot more positively than they were in the technically more sophisticated 1970s and 1980s. By then, increasingly fewer riders were able to maintain or even understand the mechanics of the bikes they rode, and only a minority would be seen alive or dead in a sidecar machine. In the words of the *Used Bike Guide* feature from 1989, the Soviet bikes "... won't do 164mph or make young women pant with lust when you approach" – fitting words upon which to end this chapter.

4 MOTORCYCLE SPORT IN THE USSR

INTRODUCTION

Motorcycle sport was varied and popular in the USSR, so a chapter such as this can give little more than an overview, the subject could easily justify a large book in its own right. Some aspects, such as road racing, off-road sport and speedway, mirror those in the West; others, such as the various ice events, are more unusual to Western observers. In the USSR the state invested heavily in sporting activity for the masses – as participants and as spectators. This arose from the belief that sporting participation made for disciplined, motivated and hard-working Soviet citizens. Mass involvement would ensure, pyramid fashion, that there would always be enough people of high

quality to be selected as an elite, and that consequential sporting success would promote communist values across the world. Although motorcycling did not enjoy the importance of the Olympic sports in this last respect, it was significant enough for Soviet participants to only move onto the world stage when they were good enough to win events and bring glory to the mother country – privateer involvement was non-existent. Given that success in motorcycling sport relied heavily on technical excellence and innovation in the machinery used, and that with the exception of defence and (associated) 'space race' production, most Soviet industry lagged behind the West in technical terms, motorcycling was unlikely to succeed as a showcase for the Soviet Union. This was unlike Olympic events, where (doping scandals aside) Soviet athletes were world beating.

SPEEDWAY

This section will start with a British connection. The sport of speedway started in Australia in the 1920s, and by the end of that decade had spread across the world, including to Great Britain. A star of those days was rider Clem Beckett from Oldham, Lancashire, who rode for various clubs,

Фиг. 20. Състезателен пистов мотоциклет ЕСО-500 см³

A Czech ESO 500cc speedway machine from the 1950s. (*Motorcycles*, 1957)

Clem Beckett, British speedway rider and communist.
(© Oldham Museum and Gallery)

Igor Plekhanov prepares for an East German speedway meeting. (From the 1964 GB Test Programme, author's collection.)

including Sheffield Tigers which he helped set up in 1929. Inspired by events in Russia that seemed to many working people to herald a new dawn for humanity, Clem became an active communist. He was instrumental in setting up a trade union for speedway riders (which earned him a ban from the sport, as, later, did a boycott of a particularly dangerous track); taking part in the 1932 Kinder Scout mass trespass, and performing on a 'Wall of Death.' In 1930, Clem took a team of riders to the Soviet Union to demonstrate speedway (as well as perform on a Wall of Death), and although it does not seem to have made any immediate impact, is mentioned here on the basis that he should be credited with introducing the sport to the USSR. Clem was killed in the Spanish Civil War fighting for his beliefs, covering the retreat of his comrades in the Jarama Valley in 1938. (Information from *Speedway Star* September 1967, and Oldham Museum and Gallery).

Speedway became big in Czechoslovakia in the 1930s, and then very popular in Poland after the war. It spread, through borrowed expertise, to the USSR in the 1950s, and teams were established across the Soviet republics, all state sponsored. A leading club, Spartak, was based in Ufa, the principal city of the Bashkir Republic, which led the sport's development in the USSR. Take-off year for competition was probably 1958, when a team from the USSR received training in Poland, and

The 1964 Soviet Speedway Team. (Author's collection)

WEST STANDING ENCLOSURE

ENTER AT **H** TURNSTILES
(See plan & conditions on back)
ENTRANCE **56**

EMPIRE STADIUM, WEMBLEY
OFFICIAL SPEEDWAY
TEST MATCH
GT. BRITAIN v U.S.S.R.
SATURDAY, JULY 4th, 1964
AT 7.15 p.m.

Price 5/-

Chairman
National League
Promoters Association

THIS PORTION TO BE RETAINED

A ticket for the first
UK/Soviet Speedway Test Match at Wembley.
(Author's collection)

The 1965 Soviet team: Back L-R: Chekranov, Fafarov, Plekhanov (Capt),
Samorodov, Volski; Front L-R: Kadirov, Kurilenko, Kadyrov.
(Author's collection)

the first major public event took place in the Lenin Stadium, Moscow. Within three years, one of these riders, Igor Plekhanov entered, and won third place in the World Championship competition in Vienna, Austria. The Soviets, of course, had access to the best machines produced by ESO, and later Jawa in Czechoslovakia.

By 1964, the USSR felt confident enough to send a test match team to the UK, where they competed against the best of Britain's riders at Wembley, Coventry and Belle Vue, introducing Soviet stars like Boris Samoridov, Gennady Kurilenko as well as Plekhanov. Not surprisingly, these newcomers trailed behind the experienced

Speedway in Riga, early 1980s. (Author's collection)

Programme, 1974 GB/USSR
speedway test match. (Author's collection)

blue-eyed boy wonder

GENNADY KURILENKO

The boy wonder of Soviet speedway and the heart-throb of the party. Blond, blue-eyed, dashing but shy . . ." Genny " is any girl's idea of a pin-up. Has been riding for the Lvov Army Club, although his spell in the Soviet forces should be over by now. Has been alternately brilliant and disappointing on previous tours, but is still rated as one of the outstanding young riders in the world today. This year, Gennady (who possesses the remarkable knack of being able to sleep ANYWHERE) seems to be in rip-roaring form. Plechanov needed a run-off to defeat him in the Soviet Championships. He won his World Championship round in Belgrade, and the semi-final at Balakowie. A great friend of Samorodov. Was once his mechanic and general " greaser ". Broke the Newport track record last season.

Kurilenko signed programme photo, 1966. (Author's collection)

UK riders, but the Soviet team won respect and admiration for its rapid rise in the sport. Further test matches followed throughout the Soviet era.

WINTER EVENTS

It would have been difficult to engage in any sporting motorcycle activity at all in the USSR's populous northern regions,

Soviet ice racing. (*Za Rulem*, January 1967)

where there are sub-zero temperatures for months on end in the winter, without racing on snow and ice, and this took various forms.

Often involving the same riders and the same tracks as speedway, 'ice speedway' caught on in the USSR, just as it had in other northern countries with harsh winter climates – but it was the Soviets who persuaded the FIM to make it a world championship sport in 1966. Ice speedway is a very exciting, highly skilled, but very dangerous sport – falling off a bike during a race can involve impalement in the spiked wheels of your own or an opponent's bike – 28mm long with typically 100 spikes on the front wheel and 150 on the rear. Machines used in the Soviet years were ESOs and Jawas, ice bikes having a more stable and rigid frame than a normal speedway machine. Unlike speedway, which involves steering and broadsiding, in ice racing the steering damper is tightened down and the bike ridden with wheels in line all the way round the track, as in road racing style. These tracks often differ in shape from the regular oval of a speedway track, having short and long straights, and varying corners. Top British-based speedway riders of the period, like Ivan Mauger, Barry Briggs and Goog Allen, all tried their hand at ice racing, with some degree of success, but it was grasstrack racer Andy Ross who achieved best performances,

Soviet lead at an international ice race meeting, 1984. (Author's collection)

BIKERNIEKU KOMPLEKSÄ SPORTA BÄZE

Motorcycle ski racing in Riga, Latvia, early 1980s. (Author's collection)

Start of the Voroshilov winter motocross event, 1950, Leningrad. (© Morton's Media)

Winter motocross, shown in *Za Rulem* February 1962 (left) and January 1977 (centre). Right: motorcycle 'mountaineering,' November 1963. (*Za Rulem*)

gaining fifth place in the World Ice Contest in 1970. However, it was the Soviets, with stars like the ethnic Tartar and speedway racer, Gab Kadyrov, who dominated the sport in these years.

Motorcycle ski racing is another sport found elsewhere in countries with harsh winters. This is possibly even more dangerous than ice speedway, involving a race on snow covered and icebound roads or lakes, where motorcycles tow skiers. Spills and broken bones seem to be frequent and accepted hazards of this sport, and the winner might be amongst the few who actually finish.

Winter motocross was a popular variant of off-road racing, but typically involved racing across snowbound courses, roads or icebound lakes, on motocross type machines. Whilst many speedway stars did ice racing in the winter, some, like Igor

Plekhanov, focused on winter motocross, which was a mass participant sport.

MOTOCROSS AND OFF-ROAD EVENTS

Off-road racing was popular across the USSR, involving, of course, little infrastructure and relatively easy adaptation of readily available lightweight road machines. There were specialist bikes developed by the major factories, some of which were entered in international endurance events, such as the ISDT (International Six Day Trial). However, these did not ultimately achieve the popularity with top riders, of the Czech Jawas and CZ machines, and (later) Austrian KTMs, which were dominant in competition across the world in the 1950s, 1960s and 1970s.

Soviet riders and teams achieved great international motocross success: in 1965,

Soviet motocross championship 1962.
(*Za Rulem,* **February 1962**)

mount, and then won his first GP race in the East German event at the end of the 1963 season. His style was admired internationally: *Motor Cycle* (3rd June, 1965) commented that Arbekov was "always in complete control of his bike, picking the smoothest path with infinite care and never seeming to deviate from it by an inch."

In 1968, the Soviet team of Arnis Angers, Evgeni Petushkov, Vladimir Pogbrniak and Leonid Shinkarenko won the Motocross des Nations held that year in the Moldovan Republic of the USSR. Guennady Moisseev from Gatchina, was FIM World 250cc Champion in 1974, 1977 and 1978, on KTM motorcycles. Moisseev was also a member of the winning Soviet team in the 1978 Motocross des Nations in West Germany, along with Vladimir Karinov, Valery Korneev, and

Victor Arbekov.
(*Za Rulem*)

Guennady Moisseev, 1977.
(*Za Rulem*)

Victor Arbekov, from Poldosk, won the FIM 250cc World Championship on a CZ. Arbekov started serious racing on a Kovrovets in the 1963 USSR 250cc GP, but finished in 4th place behind riders on CZ machines. Going on to achieve runner-up place in the Soviet championship, he was offered a Soviet team place and CZ

ИЖ-64М

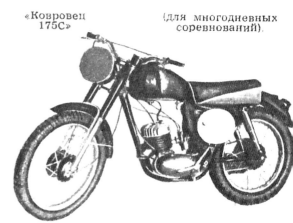

«Ковровец 175С» (для многодневных соревнований).

Kovrov motocross pennant, 1980s. (Author's collection)

Emil Forster, FIM President (centre) congratulates Boris Tramm (left) and Soviet technical supremo Alexander Skortsov after a Soviet team victory, 1964. (Author's collection)

IZH 11 competition bike. (*Za Rulem*, July 1975)

Yuri Khudiakov. After this the Soviets apparently fell out with the KTM factory, who withdrew sponsorship, and they were never again to achieve such prominence on the world stage.

Off-road racing at local and national level in the USSR could involve a large number of participants from the various clubs. British rider Olga Kevelos took part in one with other British riders in the Crimea in the late 1950s, and later remarked on this: large numbers of spectators arrived in old buses and lorries to watch an almost gladiatorial event, where riders on makeshift competition bikes, including heavyweight flat-twins, were going at such speed in the dry and dusty conditions that crashes were frequent with attendant injuries.

IZH and Kovrov competition bikes. (*Za Rulem*, May 1967)

Motoball game.
(*Za Rulem*,
November 1963)

She queried the mounting toll with Boris Tramm, top Party apparatchik in Soviet racing circles, who wryly commented that there were "plenty more where they came from!"

MOTOBALL

Motoball – playing football while riding a motorcycle in teams of five players (one of whom is in goal and not on a bike) – was apparently invented in France in the 1930s, and spread across Europe to become popular in the Soviet Union. Principal team – and the nucleus of the successful USSR national team – was 'Metallurg,' established in 1971, named and sponsored (in Soviet times, as the club still exists) by the large factory of that name in the Vidnoye District of Moscow. In Soviet times, the USSR was a regular winner of the European Championship.

ROAD RACING

Despite, in all likelihood, more technical investment than in any other area of motorcycle sport, the Soviet Union made little mark on international motorcycle road racing. It was, however, very popular, especially in Estonia, home of many of the best riders – both men and women, with the Kalev Club of Talinn and its famous trainer Tomson being dominant in the sport at club level.

Investment in technology started soon after the war within the Serpukhov factory outside Moscow, which contained a research facility devoted to such efforts using captured German technology, machines and even some personnel. Initially, and for racing within the USSR, standard motorcycles, especially large ones, were made faster with the use of superchargers – technology taken from the German factories in 1945, as described in Chapter 2. These were banned in 1951 by the FIM (the international racing body) for international competition, but not so in the Soviet Union, until it became part of the FIM in 1956.

The story of DKW input to Soviet design is speculative, as only a little is known of the peaks which the German factory had reached by the time racing development was stopped at the start of the war. Apparently, a very innovative two-stroke supercharged opposed twin engine had undergone initial development, with four pistons, and geared-together

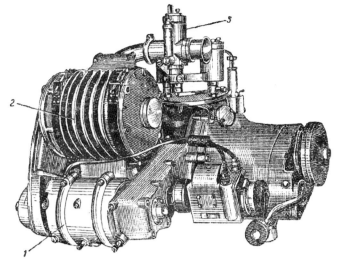

Рис. 116. Установка нагнетателя сверху двигателя мотоцикла ГК-1
1—двигатель; 2—нагнетатель; 3—карбюратор

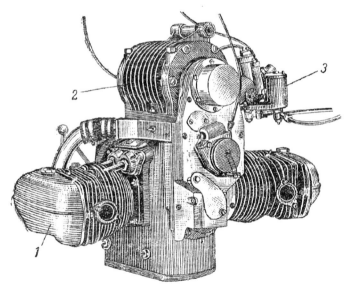

Рис. 117. Установка нагнетателя сверху двигателя М-60К:
1—двигатель; 2—нагнетатель; 3—карбюратор

Supercharged Soviet racing engines. (*Motorcycle Design*, 1953)

TK1 350cc prototype from late 1940s. (*Motorcycle Design*, 1953)

dual crankshafts. These designs formed the basis for a series of 250cc and 350cc prototypes developed from 1946, culminating with the TK1 350cc and S2B 250cc in 1949. These models were said to be capable of 47bhp and 120mph, and 40bhp and 115mph, respectively. With the ban on supercharging, this train of development was dropped. Between 1954 and 1968, effort at Serpukhov went into producing a series of road racers in sizes ranging from 125 to 500cc, which became known as Vostoks (after the rockets initially used for the very successful Soviet space programme).

The Soviets made their debut in international competition in Finland in 1956, racing S345 350cc and S555 500cc four-stroke overhead cam twin-cylinder machines. This was without success, the riders, Victor Kulakov and Nikolai Sevostianov, blaming their gearing which was unsuited to the tight circuits in that country. In 1961, a partnership with Mokotov in Czechoslovakia (makers of Jawa and CZ machines) resulted in Soviet-built copies of its successful racers – the C259 (250cc) and C360 (350cc) twin-cylinder four-strokes. The 250cc, it was claimed, produced 37bhp at 11,500rpm and 120mph, while the 350cc produced 53bhp at 10,800rpm, and 138mph on optimal gearing. These developments resulted in a hard won third place in 1961 in Helsinki, with Sevostianov riding a C360 350cc machine, and further high placings being recorded in 1962 at the East German Grand Prix 250cc and 350cc races.

In the mid-1960s the Soviets, under the directorship of I Ivanistsky and V Kuznetsov, developed their own four-cylinder racers along the lines of the latest world beating Japanese and Italian machines – the C364 (350cc) and C565 (500cc). With gear-driven double overhead camshafts and reverse cone megaphones, power output was said to be 80bhp at 12,000rpm. Despite excitement surrounding these bikes in the racing world, technical problems resulted in retirement after promising early performances. A breakthrough occurred in the 1965 East German GP,

(Continues on page 81)

GALLERY

Voskhod 2, 1972.
(Avtoexport)

IZH Jupiter, c1965.
(Vneshposyltorg)

Dnepr production in
Kiev during the 1970s.
(Avtoexport)

Minsk wedding in Dak Lak Province,
Vietnam, 5 April 2015.
(© Tuoi Tre News, Yen Thanh,
Vietnam)

IZH Planeta 3, 1972.
(Avtoexport)

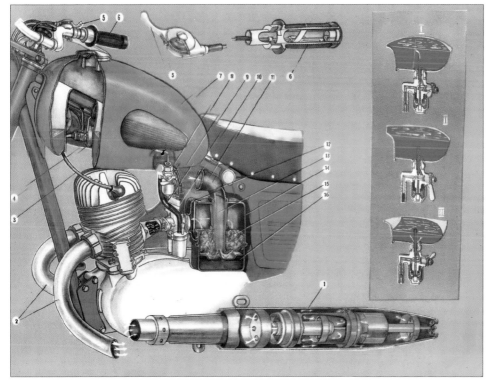

IZH Planeta 2, c1970.
(Avtoexport)

IZH Planeta 2, 1972. (Avtoexport)

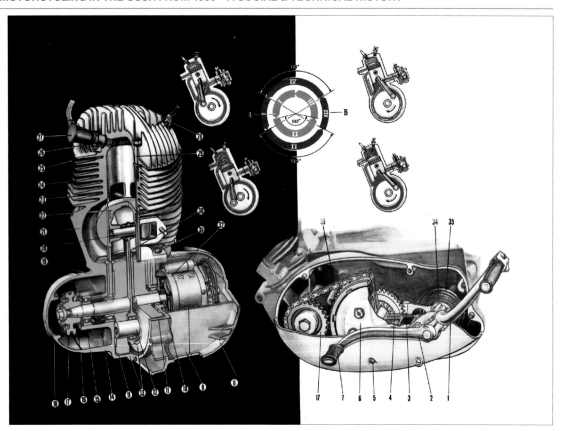

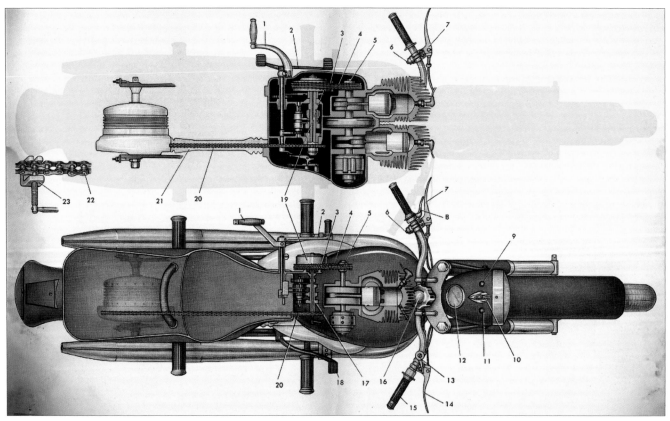

IZH Jupiter 2 and Planeta 2 compared, 1972. (Avtoexport)

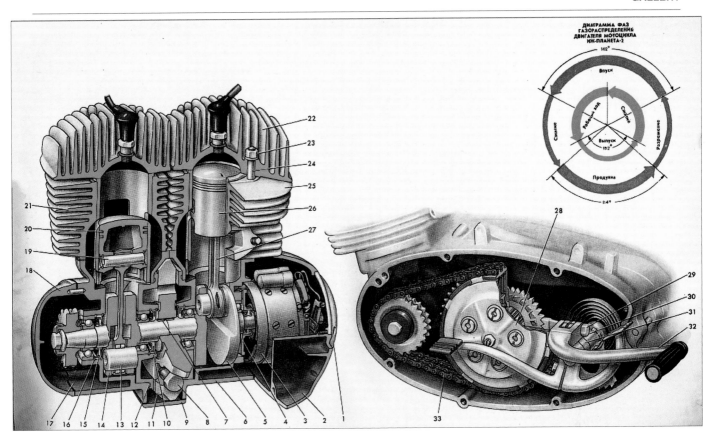

IZH Jupiter 2
engine, 1972.
(Avtoexport)

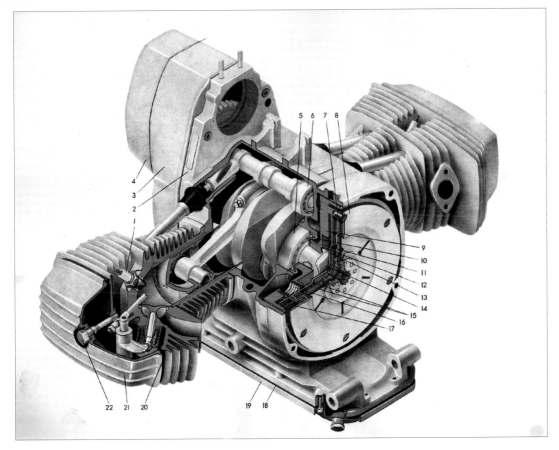

K650 engine,
c1972. (Avtoexport)

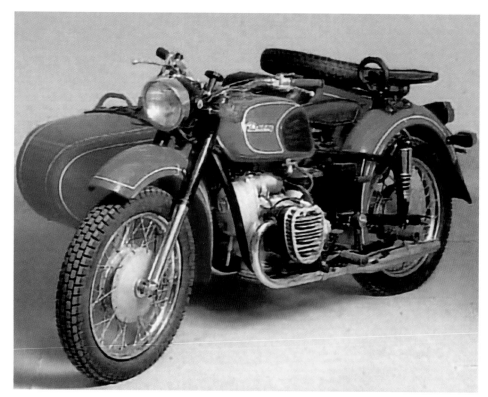

**Dnepr MT12,
c1980.
(Avtoexport)**

K650, c1972. (Avtoexport)

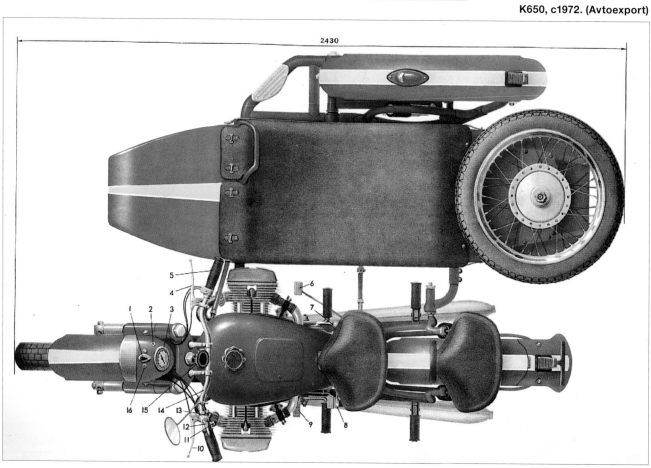

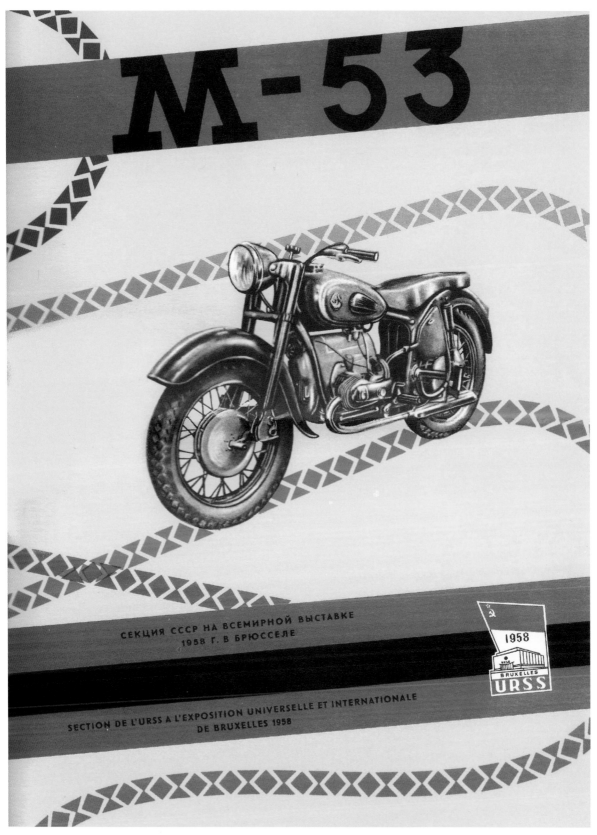

Avtoexport leaflet for M53 model for the 1958 Brussels World Fair. (Avtoexport)

The New Cossack Planeta Sport. 350cc.

The first in an exciting new generation of Soviet-built machines, the Planeta Sport 350 is stacked with style and packed with power to put you in line with the best. The only difference is that the price puts you way out ahead.

The Planeta is the only 350 bike in the U.K. with a two-stroke single-cylinder engine, which can deliver you the kind of easy cruising you've always dreamed of. Anywhere.

And its the first Soviet-built machine with direct positive oiling, and the only 2-stroke bike with an electric oil-warning light. And you get the usual Cossack comprehensive toolkit inclusive in the price. The finish is handsome—yellow and black livery with crackle-chrome mudguards.

The Planeta Sport 350 means more power for your money; and more looks for your money. And you need never tell anyone how little it cost you—they'd never believe you anyway.

Specification:

Engine. Single cylinder, 2-Stroke	Weight. 296lbs
Capacity. 340cc	Wheels. Front 300" x 19" Rear 3.50" x18"
Bore. 76mm	Suspension. Front Telescopic with Spring and Hydraulic Shock Absorbers. Rear: Swing Arm with Spring and Hydraulic Shock Absorbers.
Stroke. 78mm	
Compression. 10.1	
Power. 32 BHP-SAE	Frame. Tubular Welded.
Fuel. 93 Octane min.	
Tank. 4 gallons	
Maximum Speed. 87 mph	
Air Cleaner. Dry Paper Element	
Lubrication. Direct Injection Pump	
Battery. 12 Volt	
Ignition. Coil	
Clutch. Multi-disc, wet-type	
Gearbox. 4-speed	
Ratios. 1st: 15·34–1, 2nd: 8·78–1, 3rd: 5·9–1, 4th: 4·04–1.	
Rear Drive. Roller Bush Chain	

SATRA Cossack UK leaflet for the 350cc Planeta Sport 1975. (SATRA Belarus)

SATRA Cossack UK poster for Ural 650, c1975. (SATRA Belarus)

There's a Cossack motorcycle to turn you on. Voskhod 175cc's, 195££'s. Jupiter 350cc's, 270££'s. Ural 650cc's, 425££'s.

A Voskhod 2 pictured at the Stafford Classic Show, April 2018. This bike has only covered 35km in its lifetime. (Author)

Four-cylinder engine from a mid-1960s Vostok racer (www.cold-war-racers.com)

DOSAAF certificate for third place in a 50km 125cc race event, 1950. (Author's collection)

Programme for the August 1948 Estonian TT Road Races. (Author's collection)

1947 poster 'Long Live the All Union Day of Physical Culture' by Vladimir Krapovitsky. (Alamy Stock Images)

Sergey A Luchishkin (1902-1989):
'Parade at the Dynamo Stadium.'
IRRA (Institute of Russian Realist
Art, Moscow)

Still from *Dangerous Curves*, 1962.
(www.cold-war-racers.com)

Still from *Tulpan* movie, 2008. (Alamy Stock Images)

Znachki – Soviet era pin badges. (Author's collection)

**K750 on
exercises.
(*Za Rulem*
1967)**

Ural M67 at the harvest.
(Avtoexport)

Pannonia T20 250cc brochure in
Russian language from early 1970s.
(Author's collection)

1956 sales brochure for the C354 350cc racer. (Author's collection)

Гоночный мотоцикл С-354 предназначен для участия мотоспортсменов высокой квалификации в кольцевых шоссейных гонках.

Двигатель мотоцикла имеет высокую литровую мощность, что является одним из основных факторов, обеспечивающих значительные результаты на кольцевых гонках.

Рама мотоцикла — трубчатая, двойная, закрытого типа, обладает большой жесткостью за счет пространственного расположения труб.

Задняя подвеска выполнена в виде качающейся вилки с гидравлическими амортизаторами, что обеспечивает большой ход колеса.

Передняя вилка — телескопического типа с гидравлическими амортизаторами двойного действия, обеспечивает хорошую устойчивость мотоцикла при езде на больших скоростях.

Коробка передач — четырехступенчатая с ножным переключением.

Мотоцикл С-354 имеет сильно развитые тормозные барабаны с вентиляцией, что дает хорошую эффективность торможения.

Руль состоит из двух частей, укрепленных на верхних частях перьев вилки. Такое крепление допускает регулировку посадки водителя в широких пределах.

Седло дает возможность водителю легко изменять посадку во время езды. Удобство посадки обеспечивается также возможностью регулировки и взаимного расположения подножек и руля.

МОТОЦИКЛА С·354

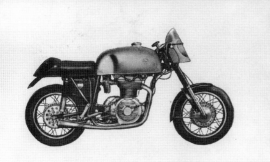

ТЕХНИЧЕСКАЯ ХАРАКТЕРИСТИКА

Общие данные. База мотоцикла — 1360 мм. Низшая точка — 157 мм. Габаритные размеры мотоцикла: длина 1984 мм, ширина 712 мм, высота 1061 мм. Вес в направленном состоянии — 165 кг. Количество мест — 1. Максимальная скорость — 155 км/час. Запас хода по топливу — 260 км.

Двигатель. Тип двигателя — четырехтактный с верхними распределительными валиками. Число цилиндров — два. Расположение цилиндров — поперечное. Диаметр цилиндра — 60 мм. Ход поршня — 61 мм. Рабочий объем цилиндров — 348 см³. Степень сжатия — 9,5. Охлаждение — воздушное. Мощность — 30 л. с. при 8000 об/мин. Система смазки — комбинированная: под давлением и разбрызгиванием.

Система питания. Емкость топливного бака — 28 л. Количество карбюраторов — два (прямоточных). Топливо — бензин с октановым числом 80. Топливный фильтр — сетчатый.

Электрооборудование. Система зажигания — двухполюсный генератор. На мотоцикле установлены катушка зажигания, распределитель, свечи.

Трансмиссия. Сцепление — многодисковое в масле. Коробка передач — четырехступенча-

тая. Переключение передач осуществляется ножным рычагом. Передаточные отношения в коробке передач:

на I-й передаче 1,83
на II-й передаче 1,31
на III-й передаче 1,09
на IV-й передаче 1,00

Передача на заднее колесо — цепью. 5/8 × 3/8". Общие передаточные числа:

на I-й передаче 10,0
на II-й передаче 7,2
на III-й передаче 6,0
на IV-й передаче 5,48

Ходовая часть. Рама — трубчатая, двойная, закрытого типа. Подвеска заднего колеса — рычажная с гидравлическими амортизаторами. Передняя вилка — телескопического типа с гидравлическими амортизаторами двойного действия. Колеса размером 18". Размер шин: 3,00—18" — передняя, 3,25—16" — задняя. Давление в шинах — 1,8 ат.

Т — 03385. Подписано к печати 3/VI 1956 г.   Тираж 15 000   Зак. 1130.
3-я типография «Красный пролетарий» Главполиграфпрома Министерства культуры СССР. Москва, Краснопролетарская, 16.

when Sevostianov came third in the 350cc race behind Jim Redman (Honda) and Derek Woodman (MZ). Disappointment, however, continued through the 1960s: despite promise and complex machinery not far behind the best innovation of the time in Japan and elsewhere, the bikes were never developed to their potential. At a time when four valve heads were being introduced, the Soviets stuck to two valves. Eventually the USSR gave up, having decided to concentrate on the smaller classes, appearing in the 1972 East German GP with 50cc and 125cc Riga machines, with seventh and eleventh places in the 50cc event. This was the last appearance of a Soviet team in world championship events.

Racing at home in the Soviet Union relied on less exotic machinery. Record-breaking developments of basic road machines of all capacities took place throughout the Soviet era, starting with the humble M1A in the late 1940s. With the larger capacity machines, racing development led to four-stroke flat-twin production, the first machines being racing ones. In 1946, the earliest M75 version used captured BMW

W Stepanov on the C254 250cc racer in 1956. (© *Speedway Star*)

**C358 350cc racer.
(Author's
collection)**

(Left) Paddock arguments look much the same anywhere: here the men in leathers are Russian riders Victor Pylaev (left) and Nicolaj Sevostjanov, who took their "350s" to the Finnish road races last May. (Above) Close-up of the "250" d.o.h.c. twin C-259 racer, seen at the Soviet Exhibition last week:

**UK coverage of the
Soviet racers in *Motor
Cycling* magazine,
13 July, 1961.
(© Morton's Media)**

R51 500cc cylinder heads on machines that were basically M72 workhorses. The later, more developed M75, followed by the M75M, M76 and M77 750cc models, continued in small scale production until the late 1950s in the Irbit factory. A parallel early postwar development was the M35 flat-twin four-stroke 350cc racer – only produced in very small numbers. The larger bikes were used extensively at

Riga racer. (www.cold-war-racers.com)

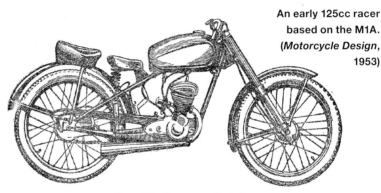

An early 125cc racer based on the M1A. (*Motorcycle Design*, 1953)

Рис. 296. Мотоцикл К-125С

Рис. 303. Мотоцикл «Комета-2»

Prototype Komet 2 supercharged 500cc racer from the late 1940s. (*Motorcycle Design*, 1953)

Рис. 301. Мотоцикл М-75

M75 750cc racer. (*Motorcycle Design*, 1953)

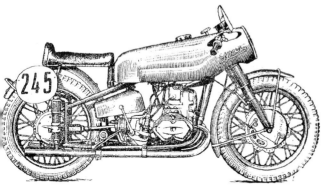

Фиг. 21. Състезателен мотоциклет М-77 („Урал")

M77 750cc racer. (*Motorcycle Design*, 1953)

Kovrovets 125cc racer. (*Za Rulem*, July 1975)

club level for both solo and sidecar racing. Other 1950s developments in Irbit were the M52 and M53 sports versions of the 500cc four-stroke flat-twins mentioned in Chapter 2. Other models were produced in prototype form over the years, but seem never to have gone into production.

The smaller two-strokes were developed for racing on home circuits, just as motocross versions were also produced.

An example was the Kovrovets SHK 175cc racer, produced at the Kovrov plant from 1964 until the late 1980s: these progressed from iron to aluminium cylinders in 1967, and a capability of 20bhp. The petrol tanks were initially derived from road ones with a crude fitment over the racing seat, but gradually developed: the last version, from 1984, had a special tank and technical innovations including reed valve intake to

Late Kovrovets SHK 175cc racer.
(www.cold-war-racers.com)

Рис. 298. Мотоцикл ИЖ-350С

Early 1950s IZH 350cc racer based on the IZH350.
(*Motorcycle Design*, 1953)

Programme for the August 1952 Estonian Road Races. (Author's collection)

A still from the 1962 film *Dangerous Curves*, set at the Tallinn Circuit. (www.cold-war-racers.com)

in 1975. These and other models were subject to racing development and tuning in late Soviet times in the Vihur works in Tallinn, Estonia.

WOMEN RACERS

As stated in the last chapter, women enjoyed notional equality in the Soviet Union, and this was certainly extended to road racing (and, to a lesser extent, off-road and ice events). Women only races at club and national level were a feature throughout the postwar Soviet period, but are reported to have disappeared with its demise. This feature of Soviet life was almost unknown in the West, where female involvement in motorcycle racing

the engine. The Izhevsk factory also produced 350cc racing models of its road bikes, from the IZH54A single cylinder in 1954, to the IZH SH12 two-cylinder

Start of a 1950s sidecar race with Kalev Club (Tallinn) trainer Tomson. (Author's collection)

Start of a 1975 event at the Tallinn circuit. (*Za Rulem*)

Top: 1974 Estonia National Road Races pennant.
Bottom: 1982 Estonia International Road Race pennant. (Author's collection)

was officially discouraged by rules that effectively barred women entrants. Stars over the years, such as Irina Ozolina, Nina Susova, Evi Nugis and the Gustel sisters (Ylme and Virve), were highly competitive racers at the top of a scene involving large numbers of women, whose times challenged the best of the men in their day. The first women's national championship race was held in Tallinn, Estonia in 1949, involving classes up to 350cc. From 1954 the championship races were all in the smaller classes with the abandonment of the 350cc event for women. The colour and spirit of women's races are wonderfully captured in the 1959 and 1961 movies *Dangerous Curves*, as will be referred to in Chapter 5 of this book.

Mullused tšempionid

Teeneline meistersportlane
I. Ozolina võitis tšempioni tiitli
125 sm³ klassis naistele.

Заслуженный мастер спорта
И. Озолина завоевала звание
чемпиона в классе 125 см³

Teeneline meistersportlane
P. Baranov võitis tšempioni
tiitli 350 sm³ klassis.

Заслуженный мастер спорта
П. Баранов завоевал звание
чемпиона в классе 350 см³

Meistersportlane N. Selivanov
võitis 125 sm³ klassis meestele
tšempioni tiitli.

Мастер спорта Н. Селиванов
завоевал звание чемпиона
в классе 125 см³

Meistersportlane G. Fomin
võitis 750 sm³ klassis
tšempioni tiitli.

Мастер спорта Г. Фомин
завоевал звание чемпиона
в классе 750 см³.

Stars of the postwar racing scene in a 1955 programme: Irina
Ozolina, P Baranov, N Selivanov and G Fomin.
(Author's collection)

Cover of the June 1955 Tallinn Race programme, showing
J Gringaut from the Moscow Club in a 750cc event.
(Author's collection)

NSV LIIDU
MEISTRIVÕISTLUSED
MOOTORISPORDIS
1955

ПЕРВЕНСТВО СССР
ПО МОТОСПОРТУ
1955

Irina Ozolina, from a 1952 race
programme. (Author's collection)

THE MOTOR CYCLE, 31 MARCH 1955

Road racing is popular in the U.S.S.R. Here is
the start of the men's race held recently at Tallinn

Women race in ice events. At a meeting earlier
this month one of the winners was M. Susova

Pictures from a March 1955 magazine report.
(*The Motor Cycle*, © Mortons Media)

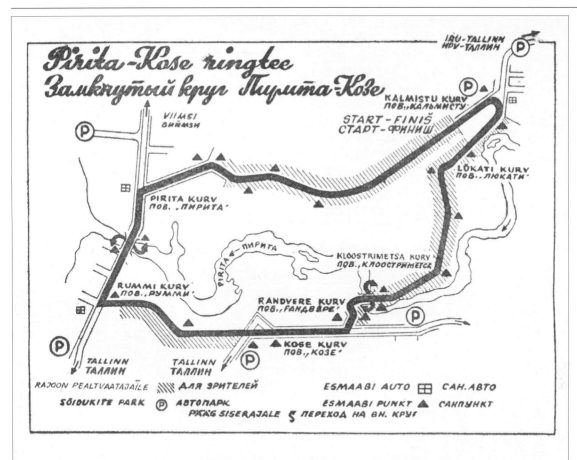

The Tallinn circuit in the Estonian SSR from the August 1952 races programme. (Author's collection)

All-round female racer Ylme Gustel in motocross event, from a 1952 race programme. (Author's collection)

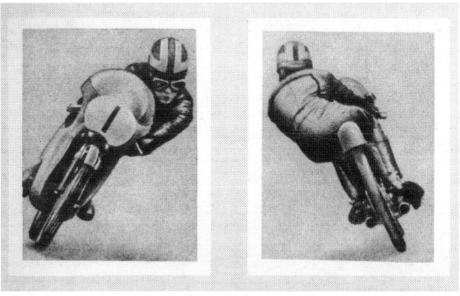

How women should corner in 50cc events. (*Za Rulem*, June 1970)

5 SOCIAL ASPECTS OF MOTORCYCLING IN THE USSR

INTRODUCTION

Given the role of planning in the development of the USSR from the time of the Revolution in 1917 onwards, Soviet history can be seen as something of a social experiment. Which bits succeeded and which failed (and which bits merely mirrored the capitalist world) will depend on the reader's politics and opinions. There can be no truly objective view for a phenomenon whose end (in the sense that what was left of the USSR and its former constituent republics abandoned any pretence of communist ideology) was so recent. Motorcycling had its place in the worlds of work, leisure and recreation in the Soviet Union, these being formulated very differently to those in more obviously market driven (and rival) capitalist societies. This chapter will examine these concepts visually through photographs from the postwar Soviet era, and the accompanying words will provide a brief context. Sport, as part of this scenario, was covered in Chapter 4.

A note on the captions: many of the images shown here are family photographs and, unless stated otherwise, are presented in the absence of known detail. Coming from sources across the former Soviet Union, many have remarkable similarities: motorcycles are often used as background props for family portraits and social occasions. The reader is asked to use their imagination to visualise the lives of the people whose images are captured in these pages.

THE WORLD OF WORK

In the socialist society that the USSR aspired to be, work was central to life, and the working class, in theory at least, the most important group in society. As we saw in Chapter 2, prices were not determined by the market, and production was planned according to need (again in theory at least). The workplace (in a society which achieved 'full' employment in 1930) fulfilled not only the need for consumption through wages, but other forms of satisfaction such as social companionship, sense of worth, and identity (Lane in

Led by a decorated 'Hero of the Soviet Union' woman, Ukrainian Kolkhoz workers head home, 1948. (Author's collection)

Kolkhoz (collective farm) workers line-up. (Author's collection)

August Kolkens Brigade leader 'Veldre' Kolkhoz, in Irlava, Latvia, with his new IZH49 in 1953.
(*Soviet Union* **English language magazine, November 1953**)

Going to work in the winter of 1956 on a Komet 125. (**Author's collection**)

Sacks and Pankhurst (eds), 1988). Initially, motorcycles were produced to get people to and from work, and as tools for work. In the period of postwar reconstruction this was all essential for economic renewal, and the countryside, where food had to be produced and transport links were poor, became an important destination for new motorcycles.

THE MILITARY

Motorcycles were extensively used by the Red Army, an institution with 5 million members in the 1980s (including the Navy and Air Force) central to Soviet life. The military, with its accompanying space programme, was the one area in which the USSR could compete effectively on the

An idealised woman worker. (*Ogonek* **magazine, 1949**)

Tips for Rural Motorcycling, 1984.
(Author's collection)

DKW 350, May Day, Lithuania, late 1940s. (Author's collection)

world stage, and lay claim to prestige and superpower status. This of course came at a price: notably low levels of investment in consumer goods, services and housing – apparently accepted by the average citizen almost until the end of the Soviet era (Jones in Sacks and Pankhurst (eds), 1988) on the basis of the need for peace and security after the devastating experience of the Great Patriotic War. Motorcycle use through to the 1980s must have exceeded that of any other army anywhere in the world, all of which is reflected in images of the time. Young men were subject to conscription and many gained their first taste of motorcycling in the army.

DOSAAF (Volunteer Society for Cooperation with the Army, Aviation, and Navy) was a mass paramilitary organisation established in 1928, whose peacetime aim was to train young people in the skills they would require for military service in wartime; membership was expected of all Komsomol (Young Communist League) members – itself virtually obligatory for young people. DOSAAF organised driving instruction as well as other skills like shooting, flying and parachuting. It organised sports events around these and other regular events, and hosted sports

Soldiers or possibly Militia (police) and IZH49. (Author's collection)

M72 in rugged military use. (Author's collection)

It wasn't all fun in the Red Army – protesters against Soviet invasion, Prague, 1968. (Photo by the late Volker Kramer)

Jawa 350 and young officers. (Author's collection)

Ural M67, 1970s. (Author's collection)

DOSAAF poster. (Author's collection)

Soyuz 6, 7 and 8 Cosmonauts parade flanked by very smart K750 escorts. (© TASS News Agency)

DOSAAF motorcycle rider's badge.

centres and gymnasiums. Motorcycling at club level in the USSR was organised through DOSAAF.

PARADES

Military-like parades to celebrate occasions such as May Day and the anniversary of

**Three-tier performing, from *Motorcyclist's Companion*, 1963.
(Author's collection)**

Athlete's parade,
Moscow Dynamo
Stadium, 1955.
(© Morton's Media)

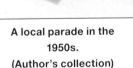

A local parade in the
1950s.
(Author's collection)

the October Revolution were widespread in the USSR, and of huge civic importance. It is said (Yurchak, 2005) that in the 1960s to 1980s period, the overwhelming majority of city-dwelling Soviet citizens either watched or participated in such parades through their social organisations (Komsomol, DOSAAF etc) – although many might not have been able to name the Politburo

A mix of machines
waiting to parade, 1970s.
(Author's collection)

Komsomol parade, 1980s. (Author's collection)

figures whose portraits they carried. Motorcycles were often used as standard bearers – a sight that seems strange to Western eyes, where motorcycles are often seen as the property of the rugged individualist (and rebel) – the antithesis of state organisation and control.

Parade at Komsomol/ DOSAAF Camp. (*Za Rulem*, 1962)

May Day parade, Riga, Latvia, 1950s. (Author's collection)

FAMILY AND LEISURE

In the 'socialist' model of the USSR, leisure activities were organised collectively, and, although choices were available, individualism was not encouraged. Activities that were sponsored by the state promoted collective endeavour and social contribution, and it was not until the 1960s that consumers themselves were trusted as, by now, fully developed Soviet citizens, to determine for themselves, through purchase of goods and services, how they wanted to spend their time and surplus wages outside work (Koenker, 2013). Motorcycles did not have the same connotations of youthful rebellion that

Prewar L300. (Author's collection)

A family with its K750 and sidecar. (Author's collection)

A 1950s Ukraine picnic spot scene with military-style attired sidecar machine owners. (Author's collection)

A family with its bald-tyred M72 and sidecar. (Author's collection)

Men pick flowers for their wives on a motorcycle outing. (Author's collection)

A K175 and Gaz-24 Volga car in Stavropol, SW Russia, 1964. (Author's collection)

they had in the West – at least not until the Planeta Sport model came along in the 1970s, offering young Soviets a taste of what was available to their contemporaries in the capitalist world. That embryonic youth culture is reflected in some of the photographs here. With cars being unaffordable, motorcycles, especially those with sidecars, were widely used for family transport long after they disappeared as such from roads in the UK and Western Europe (they remained popular in South East Asia). Travel for its own sake – rather than to attend a distant holiday sanatorium (a Soviet Union workers' rest and recuperation centre) – grew from the 1960s onwards, the Black Sea resorts being favourite destinations for holidays (Koenker, 2013). The roads were poor and petrol stations few, and most people still travelled longer distances by train: such a journey by road would involve detailed preparation, planning, and ultimate adventure.

M72 and sidecar, 1954. (Author's collection)

Family photo with IZH49, 1950s.
(Author's collection)

K175B with an IZH front mudguard – it must have arrived at this beauty
spot three-up. (Author's collection)

K55 125cc being pushed onto the beach by the wife, whilst husband
takes photo, Latvia, 1959. (Author's collection)

Another IZH49, with posing girlfriend.
(Author's collection)

Komet K125 and children, 1957. (Author's collection)

Fettling a Voskhod 2 in the sunshine. (Author's collection)

Fixing an IZH49 that appears to be sinking. (Author's collection)

Za Rulem (translates as 'Behind the Steering Wheel') was the mass circulation motoring magazine in the Soviet Union. It started in 1928 and continues to this day in Russia, now in private ownership. During the period under examination it was a 30-page, well-illustrated magazine, covering all aspects of motoring (including motorcycling), with reviews of the latest models, technical articles, and coverage of sporting events (see examples on page 106).

The Soviet motorcyclist was well served by motorcycling technical literature. Whilst home maintenance was essential given the dearth of servicing facilities, books were cheap and in plentiful supply in the USSR (the biggest volume publisher in the world in its day). Although printing quality was poor and photographs not always well presented, the books offered comprehensive and well-illustrated guides to the rider and home mechanic – examples have featured elsewhere in this book. One notable book (*Motorcyclist's Companion*)

Two photographs of a family picnic – with the young boys far more interested in the K750 and sidecar than the dancing. (Author's collection)

from 1963 was the perfect DOSAAF manual – with instruction on subjects as diverse as carrying wounded soldier comrades on a solo machine, to stunt riding, parade showmanship, all the various motorcycle sports, and camping. Of exceptionally high quality were the large (28 x 42cm) coloured albums with 3D cutaway diagrams released for a short period in the 1970s; at least one in multilingual form under the

K1B 98cc passes the house
two-up at speed. (Author's collection)

Echoes of American counter-culture in this portrait from the
1950s/1960s period. (Author's collection)

IZH350 back from a hunting expedition. (Author's collection)

M72 with sidecar, and fisherman at rest. (Author's collection)

Ural M63 with fisherman and catch. (Author's collection)

Avtoexport label (illustrations from these are featured in Chapter 2 and the colour gallery, pages 67-69).

While there are numerous photographs amongst the author's collection of women posing on machines, there are few from the postwar period featuring women riders (one appeared earlier in this chapter). In theory, women and men enjoyed equality in the USSR, but, under the surface, Soviet society was as patriarchal as that in the West – gender stereotyping proved very resistant to change (Sacks in Sacks and Pankhurst (eds), 1988).

IZH Planeta, Estonia, where suitcases are seen as symbolic of war, occupation and dislocation. (Author's collection)

IZH49 and owner, 1957. (Author's collection)

IZH49 and posing woman, 1950s.
(Author's collection)

Polished and proud: IZH56, 1958. (Author's collection)

IZH49 machines at a festival in Latvia.
(Author's collection)

Ural motorcycle at Novosibirsk Station, Western Siberia.
(Author's collection)

Summer pleasures. (Author's collection)

'Wild' youth with transistor radio and
Kovrovets 175, Ukraine. (Author's collection)

IZH machines and either summer rain or mosquitoes,
Kharkov, Ukraine. (Author's collection)

Picnic party with
various bikes
including a Planeta
Sports. (Author's
collection)

Planetas out for a run. (Author's collection)

Jupiter and sidecar, Tashkent, Uzbekistan. (Author's collection)

Leaving for holiday on Jawa and Voskhod machines. (Author's collection)

Young couple and Voskhod 2. (Author's collection)

Young people from Stavropol, SW Russia, with Planeta Sport. (Author's collection)

On holiday from Novosibirsk, Western Siberia. (Author's collection)

Voskhod and Jawa bikes on river ferry. (Author's collection)

Riders from Pskov enter Yaroslavl Region on their Jawas. (Author's collection)

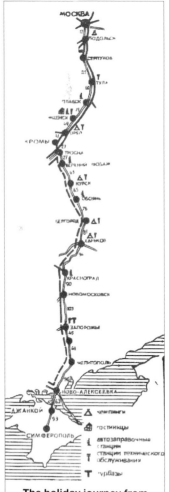

The holiday journey from Moscow to the Crimea, showing campsites, hostels, petrol stations and tourist centres. (*Motorcycle Tourist's Companion*)

The same group at Plavsk, south of Moscow, and perhaps en-route to the Crimean coast – a very long journey from Pskov. (Author's collection)

Za Rulem, August 1969 (left) and March 1983 (right).

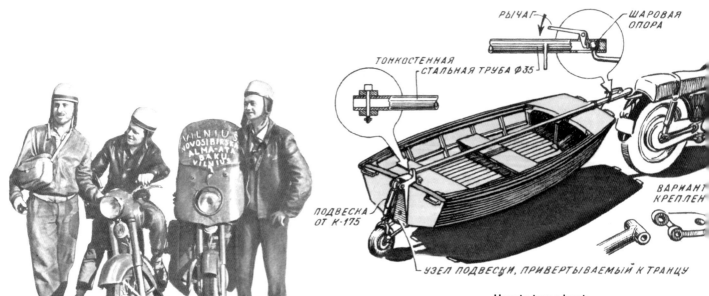

Vilnius to Baku trip by Jawa, *Za Rulem*,
November 1963.

How to tow a boat.
(*Za Rulem*, February 1962)

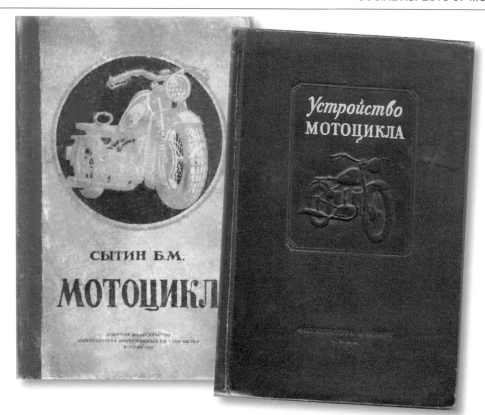

Motorcycle – all military types, including UK and US, manual 1947 (left), and *Motorcycle Design*, 1953.

Motorcycle Companion, 1963.

Instructional drawing from *Motorcycle Companion*.

During the Great Patriotic War, women endured the same hardships and fighting roles as did men (although in far fewer numbers), but after the war were almost excluded from the military. They remained however, both educated for, and working across the full range of occupations in

Modern Motorcycles, Moscow, 1958.

Фиг. 209. Последици от неспазване на правилата за движение

How to have an accident in town – from *Motorcycles*, Moscow, 1958.

Motorcycles (in Bulgarian but printed in Moscow) 1957.

Avtoexport IZH, all colour large format book c1970.

civilian life. In postwar Soviet Union they were expected to work (with good childcare provision by the state, which wanted to see an increase in the birthrate), but also had to undertake all the traditional domestic chores at home. It seems that few had the time or inclination for motorcycling. Sport, however, as we saw in Chapter 4, certainly included women, and on a scale in some areas never seen in the West.

Young lady on a IZH56. (Author's collection)

Female rider on an M103 125cc in the British press. (*Motor Cycling*, 1961 © Morton's Media)

ENTERTAINMENT: THE WALL OF DEATH AND THE CIRCUS

The 'Wall of Death,' which originated in the USA, became a popular carnival entertainment in the 1920s and '30s, and reached the USSR. Motorcycles run at increasing speed horizontally round and round a drum-like cylinder made of wood, and the riders perform stunts for the audience who stand around the top of the 'wall' on a tiered platform. A famous Soviet performer was Natalia Androsova, who was actually related to the former, executed Czar. From the late 1930s until the 1950s, broken only by the war and adventurous military service, she wowed the crowds in Moscow's Gorky Park and even drew the admiration of a famous poet Andrei Voznesenskiy who wrote of her:

Natalia Androsova, 'Wall of Death' rider. (Unknown origin)

The motorcycle a chainsaw over her head,
Tired of living upright.
Ah, wild soul, daughter of Icarus.

The Filatov Bear Show at the Moscow State Circus, 1964. (© TASS News Agency)

Circuses are traditional forms of entertainment in Russia and Eastern Europe. A famous circus family in the Soviet Union era were the Filatovs, who trained large animals including brown bears that rode motorcycles. The Filatov Circus has survived Soviet times and continues, controversially, in Russia today.

ART AND CULTURE

Motorcycles have featured in state-sponsored art and cultural media since the early years of the USSR. The favoured art form in the Soviet Union was 'socialist realism,' and examples are to be found in monument form throughout the former Soviet Union and Eastern Europe, including the war memorial in Sofia, Bulgaria, shown in Chapter 1. Motorcycles often featured in posters and paintings in the socialist realist style. Motorcycle images of sporting machines were sometimes used on postage stamps and 'QSL cards' (proof of reception sent to listeners by international short wave radio stations). The USSR also produced pin badges ('Znachki') prolifically that celebrated Soviet life and history, and there were numerous designs featuring sporting events and motorcycle use (see Gallery, page 78).

Motorcycles were central to at least one movie: *Dangerous Curves*, made in the

Rodchenko Linear Construction, pre- socialist realist artwork, 1933. (Unknown origin)

Tallinn Studios, Estonia in 1959, and then remade with slight changes, in wide-format colour in 1962. This comedy's plot revolves around identical twin sisters, one of whom is a motorcycle racer in the local club in Tallinn. The sisters swap places and all sorts of funny mishaps take place around

Postcard image: 'Motorcycle Race on Saturn' Kolya Zapryagaev (13yrs), children's competition entry, 1962. (Author's collection)

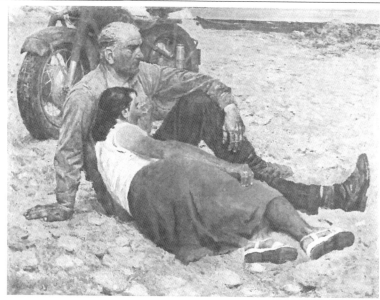

Postcard image: 'The Lovers' (1959) by Geliy Korzhev (1925-2012). (Author's collection)

Postcard image: 'Motorcycle Racers' (1970). (Author's collection)

Radio QSL postcard from 1967. (Author's collection)

male suitors, two of whom are rival racers. This is a superb film with great racing scenes on the road circuit in Tallinn, and a countryside scene involving an IZH56 350cc that is slapstick at its best. Being a Soviet film, the dock-working racer, rather than his white collar-rival, gets the girl.

Another movie which features a scene with an unusual Soviet era working motorcycle was the drama *Tulpan,* made in Kazakhstan in 2008, which centres on the way of life of nomadic herders. This involves the visit of a travelling vet mounted on a Ural combination, with a sick baby camel in the sidecar whose angry mother is in hot pursuit (see Gallery, page 78).

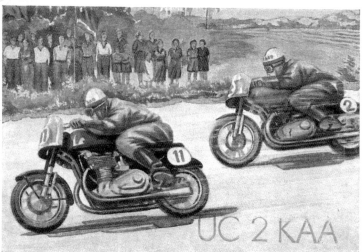

ОВЛАДЕВАЙТЕ ИСКУССТВОМ ВОЖДЕНИЯ МОТОЦИКЛА!

USSR postwar postage stamps. (Author's collection)

Still from *Dangerous Curves* 1962.
(www.cold-war-racers.com)

PAPERS AND BUREAUCRACY

This was no different in reality to that in Western countries, despite the enduring image of Soviet bureaucracy and state policing. In addition to identity papers, Soviet riders were required to register their vehicles and carry an appropriate licence. The Militia (police force) was considered a nuisance – but then that is probably universal!

1962 Yugoslav poster for *Dangerous Curves* movie. (Author's collection)

Soviet motorcycle licence cover.
(Author's collection)

Top left: Tashkent-issued motorcycle licence inside cover from 1959.
Top right: Soviet motorcycle registration document cover. Left: Soviet
registration document inside cover for MT10-36 motorcycle. Above:
Registration document details for M104 motorcycle. (Author's collection)

MOTORCYCLE IMPORTS

Motorcycles from Eastern European countries within the Soviet Bloc were imported to the USSR throughout the Soviet era. Some, like Czech Jawa 350cc models, were very popular, and apparently purchased in large numbers, although they were said to suffer from the poor quality two-stroke fuel mixture available in the USSR. On the rarer side was a batch of 1000 East German AWO 425cc four-stroke singles, imported in 1950 before agreement was reached (or orders were issued!) that this factory would produce only two-stroke machines. Less common than the Jawa, but also popular, were the Hungarian Pannonia 250cc two-stroke bikes made from the early 1950s until 1975. There

Militia papers inspection, *Za Rulem*, November 1963.

Former Odessa Region Partisan Fighter Melanija Petrova on back of captured BMW R35, postwar. (Author's collection)

BMW R12 still in use in Latvia, 1959. (Author's collection)

Rare East German (DDR) AWO425 in the USSR. (Author's collection)

BMW R12 in the USSR. (Author's collection)

NSU 251 OSL from the early 1930s in the USSR. (Author's collection)

Jawa 350 in the 1970s. (Author's collection)

were, of course, a number of less official imports of motorcycles, either seized in the Soviet-occupied part of Germany at the end of the war, or left by the Nazi occupying forces as they retreated in advance of the Red Army from 1943 onwards.

THE END OF THE SOVIET PERIOD

The reforms of the late 1980s under Gorbachev led to the end of the Soviet socialist project, and establishment of completely separate states in most of the former republics. This was driven by a complicated and interrelated series of events, including moves for reform in Poland and elsewhere, the long, drawn-out and unsuccessful war in Afghanistan (along with the expense of the arms

Another of the popular Jawa two-stroke bikes. (Author's collection)

И. ДОЧКАЛ
ОБСЛУЖИВАНИЕ
И РЕМОНТ
МОТОЦИКЛОВ
ЯВА

Jawa manual in Russian language covering all models to 1987. (I Dockal, 1987)

Jawa 350, from a factory brochure. (Author's collection)

Jawa with sidecar in family use. (Author's collection)

Customised Jawa in 1980s USSR.
(Author's collection)

A Pannonia two-stroke in the USSR. (Author's collection)

race with the USA), and the Chernobyl disaster which shook faith in the infallibility of socialist technology. One by one, the satellite states in Eastern Europe quickly 'freed' themselves from communist forms of government. This also heralded an end to state ownership, and much 'birth to grave' state provision – no longer was work and basic income in Russia and the former USSR republics guaranteed. Clever entrepreneurs took advantage of the economic dislocation, and bought up sections of highly profitable state enterprises, notably gas and oil production,

Pannonia T20 engine detail, from the factory brochure. (Author's collection)

КАРБЮРАТОР

Двигатель имеет два карбюратора с центральной поплавковой камерой и воздушным корректором. Центральное расположение поплавковой камеры обеспечивает неизменность состава горючей смеси и в мотоцикле, наклонном в сторону.
В комплект карбюратора входят воздухоочистители с глушителями шума всасывания.

Технические данные карбюраторов

Число карбюраторов	2	Жиклер холостого хода	0,50 мм
Тип карбюратора	П20	Жиклер дополнительного	
Диаметр проходного сечения	Ø 20 мм	воздуха	1,30 мм
Главный жиклер	0,80 мм	Жиклер корректора	0,60 мм
Распылитель	2,60 мм		

СЦЕПЛЕНИЕ

Сцепление масляное, дисковое, с пробковыми накладками. Оно получает привод от коленчатого вала через косозубую шестеренчатую передачу.
Сцепление и коробка передач имеют общую масляную ванну.

creating a new class of 'oligarchs' in Russia. Whilst there was mass support for the introduction of the market across the whole economy, it did result in unemployment and uncertainty for many, as change became consolidated in the 1990s. For motorcycling this meant that as the market was no longer under state control, motorcyclists could buy Western and Far Eastern models if they had the cash: no longer were products generally regarded as plain and technologically inferior, the only ones available. As documented in Chapter 2, this resulted in the end of several of the motorcycle plants, including, notably, the Dnepr Factory (KMZ) in Kiev, Ukraine (which was now in the fully independent Republic of Ukraine). The IMZ Irbit plant producing Ural machines also suffered: after two bankruptcies in the post-Soviet period it was purchased by

three US-based Russian entrepreneurs in 2000: its survival depended on the closure of most of the plant, disposal of most of the workforce, and continued production, with components sourced worldwide, aimed predominantly at a high-end US market of older riders with large disposable incomes.

Socially, the new states could not provide the level of subsidised mass leisure and cultural opportunity that had been available in the USSR, and this saw the end of organised motorcycle leisure activity through DOSAAF clubs. From now on, Western influence, including the growth of such phenomena as motorcycle gang culture, as well as markets dictated by fashion and consumer choice (for those who could afford it), would predominate. 'Really existing socialism' (as it was known by its advocates in the 1960s) was at an end.

The well-dressed Soviet motorcyclist, from the 1963 *Motorcycle Companion* book, Moscow, 1963.

APPENDIX 1

POSTWAR MOTORCYCLE, SCOOTER, MOPED & CYCLE MOTOR PRODUCTION IN THE USSR

Model	Year(s)	Factory	Capacity (cc)	Cylinders	Valve position	Power (bhp)
M72	1941-62	Postwar: Irbit, Gorky & Kiev	746	Flat-twin	SV	22.0
K1B	1946-50	Kiev	98	Single	Two-stroke	2.3
M1A	1946-56	Moscow (1946-1951) Minsk (from 1951)	123.2	Single	Two-stroke	4.75
K125	1946-60	Kovrov	123.2	Single	Two-stroke	4.75
IZH 350	1947-51	Izhevsk	346.1	Single	Two-stroke	11.5
IZH 49	1951-58	Izhevsk	346.1	Single	Two-stroke	11.5
M31	1954	Serpukhov/Minsk	350	Single	OHV	18
IZH 56	1956-62	Izhevsk	346.1	Single	Two-stroke	13.0
K55	1956-58	Kovrov	123.2	Single	Two-stroke	4.75
K58	1958-60	Kovrov	123.2	Single	Two-stroke	5.0
M101 M103	1958-64 1961-64	Minsk	123.2	Single	Two-stroke	5.0
K175 K175A	1957-59 1959-62	Kovrov	173.7	Single	Two-stroke	8.0
M52 M53	1956-59	Irbit	494	Flat-twin	OHV	25.0 28.0
M61 M62	1958-60 1960-65	Irbit	649	Flat-twin	OHV	28.0
K750 Dnepr MW 750M	1959-77 1964-77	Kiev	746	Flat-twin	SV	26.0
Spriditis moped	1959-61	Riga	60	Single	Two-stroke	1.5
Riga 1 moped	1961-65	Riga	49.8	Single	Two-stroke	1.5
Gauja Cyclemotor	1961-66	Penza	45	Single	Two-stroke	1.0
VP 150 scooter	1957-66	Vyatskiye Polyany	145.45	Single	Two-stroke	5.0
T 200 scooter	1957-62	Tula	199	Single	Two-stroke	8.0
T200M	1962-67	Tula	199	Single	Two-stroke	9.0
IZH Jupiter Jupiter 2	1961-70 1970-71	Izhevsk	347	Twin	Two-stroke	19.0
IZH Planeta Planeta 2	1962-66 1966-71	Izhevsk	346.1	Single	Two-stroke	13.0 15.5
K175B	1962-63	Kovrov	173.7	Single	Two-stroke	9.0
K175W Voskhod	1963-70	Kovrov	173.7	Single	Two-stroke	10.0
M104	1965-69	Minsk	123.2	Single	Two-stroke	5.5
M63 Ural	1965-70	Irbit	649	Flat-twin	OHV	28.0
M66 Ural	1968-75	Irbit	649	Flat-twin	OHV	30.0
Riga 3 moped	1965-69	Riga	49.8	Single	Two-stroke	2.0
VP150M scooter	1966-73	Vyatskiye Polyany	148	Single	Two-stroke	6.0
Tourist Tourist M	1968-78	Tula	199	Single	Two-stroke	11.0
MP 043 MP 054 mopeds	1969	Lvov	50	Single	Two-stroke	2.0 4.0

Model	Year(s)	Factory	Capacity (cc)	Cylinders	Valve position	Power (bhp)
Riga 4 moped	1970-74	Riga	49.9	Single	Two-stroke	2.0
K650 Dnepr MT9	1967-77 1971-76	Kiev	649	Flat-twin	OHV	32.0
M105 M106	1969-74	Minsk	123.2	Single	Two-stroke	7.0
Voskhod 2 2M	1970-77 1977-80	Kovrov	173.7	Single	Two-stroke	10.5 14.0
Planeta 3	1971-75	Izhevsk	346.1	Single	Two-stroke	18.0
Jupiter 3 Jupiter 3K	1970-80	Izhevsk	347	Twin	Two-stroke	25.0
Planeta Sport	1974-83	Izhevsk	340	Single	Two-stroke	30.0
Vyatskiye 3 Electron scooter	1974-79	Vyatskiye Polyany	148	Single	Two-stroke	7.0
Verkhovina 4 Verkhovina 5 mopeds	1973 1975-79	Lvov	49.8	Single	Two-stroke	2.0
Riga 5 Riga 7 mopeds	1966-75 1973-79	Riga	45	Single	Two-stroke	1.0
Riga 12 moped	1974-79	Riga	49.9	Single	Two-stroke	2.2
M67 Ural M67-36	1972-76 1976-83	Irbit	649	Flat-twin	OHV	32.0 36.0
MT10 Dnepr MT 10-36	1973-76 1976-78	Kiev	649	Flat-twin	OHV	32.0 36.0
Minsk 125	1974	Minsk	123.2	Single	Two-stroke	8.0
MT12 Dnepr	1977-85	Kiev	746	Flat-twin	SV	26.0
Tulitsa Tulitsa 02M scooters	1978-83 1983-91	Tula	199	Single	Two-stroke	14 14.5
Voskhod 3 Voskhod 3M	1980-83 1983-89	Kovrov	173.7	Single	Two-stroke	14.0
Werchowina 6 moped	1979	Lvov	49.8	Single	Two-stroke	2.2
Riga 16 Riga 22 mopeds	1978-84 1982-87	Riga	45	Single	Two-stroke	1.3
Jupiter 4	1981-85	Izhevsk	347	Twin	Two-stroke	28.0
MMVZ 3.112 MMVZ 3.115	1976-89	Minsk	123.2	Single	Two-stroke	12.0
Planeta 4	1982-87	Izhevsk	346.1	Single	Two-stroke	20.0
MT11 Dnepr MT16 Dnepr	1981-	Kiev	649	Flat-twin	OHV	32.0
M67-6 (IMZ 8.103)	1983-	Irbit	649	Flat-twin	OHV	34.0
Jupiter 5	1985-	Izhevsk	347.6	Twin	Two-stroke	24.0
Planeta 5	1987-	Izhevsk	346.1	Single	Two-stroke	22.0
Riga Mini Mini-moped	1984-	Riga	49.9	Single	Two-stroke	1.8

Notes:

1. Motorcycle unless otherwise described in first column.
2. Years are approximate as there were overlaps, and production commencement did not always take place as planned.
3. In Chapter 2 standard motorcycle production in postwar USSR was described as belonging to three 'families.' These are shaded accordingly in the table: the 125cc and 175cc two-stroke singles (light grey), the 350cc two-stroke singles and twins (mid grey), and the larger capacity flat (or boxer) overhead valve twins (dark grey).
4. SV = side valve, OHV = overhead valve.

APPENDIX 2
IMAGE SOURCES, BIBLIOGRAPHY & WEBSITES

NOTE ON IMAGE SOURCES

Every effort was made by the author to establish the origin of photographs known to have been published previously, and all images used are credited where this has been possible. Many of the photographs are from private sources and have not been published before – these are shown as from the 'author's collection.' The origins of some, particularly wartime ones, are unknown, but are believed to originate from official Soviet state sources, and have been published elsewhere. Some image sources have been quoted, but it has proved impossible to track down the individual concerned to obtain permission for use – if any individual feels their work has been used without their authority, this has been quite unintentional and the author should be contacted via the publisher so that the matter can be resolved properly.

Particular thanks for use of images should go to the UK magazine *Speedway Star*, the UK magazine *Superbike* which is now online (www.superbike.co.uk), the *Institute of Russian Realist Art* (IRRA) Moscow, Morton's Media Ltd, Alan Voase (of the former *Neval Motorcycles*), Russian motoring magazine *Za Rulem,* Tuoi Tre News (Vietnam), Martijn Stehouwer (www.cold-war-racers.com) and the Cossack Owners' Club. Some advice was provided directly by Chris Tomes of *Vostok Motorcycles* (Soviet era motorcycle parts suppliers): www.facebook.com/vostokmotorcycles.co.uk) and Andrey Semochkin (Mel) from Moscow.

BOOKS

Alexievich, S. (2016) *Second Hand Time* London: Fitzcarraldo.
Bacon, R. (1979) *Foreign Racing Motorcycles* Sparkford: Haynes.
Bacon, R. (1985) *Military Motorcycles of World War 2* London: Osprey.
Bacon, R. (1986 revised edition) *BMW Singles and Twins* London: Osprey.
Dockal, I. (1987) *Jawa Motorcycles Service and Repair* (Russian Language book) Moscow.
Garant (2017) *Zweirader aus dem Osten* Renningen: Garant.
Goldman, Anke-Eva *Soviet Racing Women* https://thevintagent.com/2017/07/02/anke-eve-goldmann-soviet-racing-women/
Gusek, Pavel. (1981) *World Championship Motocross Motorcycles* (Russian Language book) Moscow.
Heavy Motorcycles (Russian Language book) (1976) Moscow – 2-52.
Hobsbaum, E. (1995) *The Age of Extremes – The Short 20th Century 1914-1991* London: Abacus
Hosking, G. (1985) *A History of the Soviet Union* London: Fontana
Inkeles, A and Geiger, K. (eds) (1961) *Soviet Society – A Book of Readings* Boston: Houghton Mifflin.
Koenker, D. (2013) *Vacation, Travel and the Soviet Dream* Ithaca NY: Cornell University Press.
K125 and K175 Motorcycles (Russian Language book) (1966) Moscow.
Lewin, M. (2005) *The Soviet Century* London: Verso.
Mason, N. (2012) *100%* Yorkshire: Nev Mason Books.
Motorcycles (Bulgarian Language book)

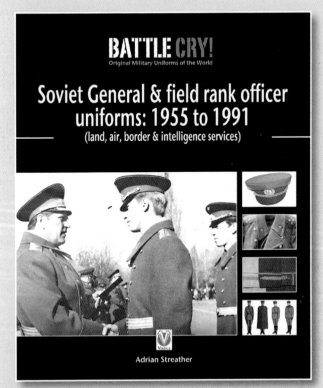

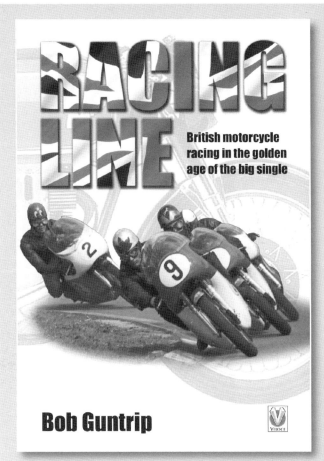

Bob Guntrip

Racing Line is the story of big-bike racing in Britain during the 1960s – when the British racing single reached its peak; when exciting racing unfolded at circuits across the land every summer; and when Britain took its last great generation of riding talent and engineering skill to the world.

ISBN: 978-1-845847-93-7
Hardback • 22.5x15.2cm • 232 pages
• 76 colour and b&w pictures

"One of the finest records I have ever read of the unforgettable 1960s racing era ..."
(Old Bike Mart)

Until now, Gary Hocking was the only World Motorcycle Champion of his era without a book dedicated to his life. This book reveals Gary's life in Rhodesia, how he was helped to become a World Champion, his dedication, and retirement at a young age – and the accident that cost him his life.

ISBN: 978-1-787114-14-2
Hardback • 21x14.8cm • 176 pages
• 70 pictures

"This is a thoroughly fascinating and interesting book about a long forgotten champion and I thoroughly recommend it."
(On the Level)

For more information and price details see veloce.co.uk • email info@veloce.co.uk • tel: +44(0)1305 260068

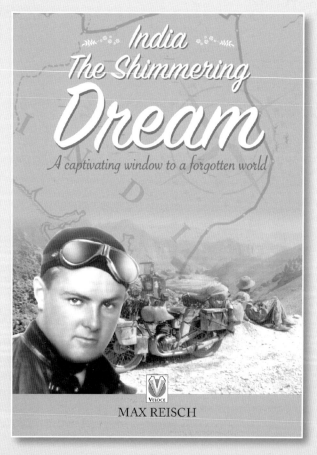

INDEX

Androsova, Natalia 109
Angers, Arnis 61
Arbekov, Victor 61
Avtoexport 45, 46, 50, 101
AWO 32, 113, 114

Ballard, Peter 5, 8, 10,
Beckett, Clem 55, 56
Beryozka 33, 47, 48
BMW 10-12, 17, 18, 23, 28, 37, 39, 41,
    50-52, 54, 81, 114
Bulgaria 19, 110, 122

Circus(es) 7, 110
Cold war 9, 19, 54
Cossack 5, 47, 48, 50, 72
Cossack Owners' Club 5, 121, 122
Czech/Czechoslovakia 7, 28, 52, 56, 57, 60,
    64, 113

Dangerous Curves (movie) 77, 84, 85, 112
DKW 12, 14, 21, 25, 28, 39, 41, 50, 109, 119
Dnepr (models) 27, 42-44, 49
DOSAAF 74, 91-95, 100, 118

German(y) 7-12, 14, 15, 17, 19, 21, 22, 24,
    27, 28, 32, 39, 41, 50, 56, 61, 63, 64, 81,
    113-115
GMZ 22
Gorbachev, Mikhail 115
Gorky 22, 25, 28, 39, 41, 50, 109, 119
Gustel, Virve 85
Gustel, Ylme 85, 87

Hungary/Hungarian 7, 113

Ice speedway 59
Irbit 21-27, 39, 41-44, 50, 82, 83, 118-120

Ivanistsky, I 65
IZH (models) 12, 24, 32-36, 48, 50, 62, 65,
    67-69, 102, 103, 108, 119
Izhevsk 10, 12, 21, 22, 24, 25, 35-37, 44, 50,
    82, 83, 118-120

Jawa 28, 35, 52, 53, 92, 105, 106, 113, 115,
    116, 121
Jupiter 35-37, 46, 47, 50, 51, 65, 68, 69,
    104, 119

K750 38, 39, 41, 46, 79, 96, 120
Karinov, Vladimir 61
Khrushchev, Nikita 21
Khudiakov, Yuri 62
Kiev 21, 22, 25-27, 39, 42, 43, 49, 66,
    118-120
KMZ 25, 41, 43, 44, 49, 118
Komsomol 91, 94, 95
Korneev, Valery 61
Kovrov 21, 22, 26, 29, 30-32, 35, 44, 62, 83,
    119, 120
Kovrovets 32, 50, 61, 83, 84, 103
Kulakov, Victor 64
Kurilenko, Gennady 57
Kuznetsov, V 64

M72 10-12, 17, 19, 22, 23, 25, 26, 28, 36-41,
    50, 82, 92, 96
Mason, Nev 22, 49, 50, 52, 54, 121
Minsk 21, 22, 26, 27, 29-32, 47, 49, 50, 52,
    54, 66, 119, 120
MMZ 26, 27, 49
Moisseev, Guennady 61
Motoball 63
Motocross 61, 121
Movies 110, 111
Mukhin, Pyotr 38, 39, 41

Neval 49, 50, 52, 53, 121
NSU 17-19, 115
Nugis, Evi 85

Ozolina, Irina 85, 86

Pannonia 80, 113, 117
Parades 7, 93, 94
Petushkov, Evgeni 61
Planeta 33-35, 37, 47, 50, 67, 68, 72, 97,
    102-104, 119, 120
Planeta Sport 33, 34, 72, 97, 103, 104, 120
Plekhanov, Igor 56, 57, 60
PMZ 8, 12
Pogbrniak, Vladimir 61
Poland 8, 29, 56, 115

Raccoons 44
Road racing 63, 64, 82-87

Samoridov, Boris 57
SATRA 47-49, 52
Serpukhov 22, 25, 27, 32, 63, 64, 119
Sevostianov, Nikolai 64, 81
Shinkarenko, Leonid 61
Sidecars 5, 7, 10, 11, 26, 28, 33, 35, 38-41,
    43, 44, 48, 50-52, 54, 83, 85, 96-98, 100,
    101, 104, 111, 116
Ski (motorcycle) racing 59, 60
SMZ 27

Speedway 56-58, 81, 121
Susova, Nina 85

TIZ 12, 13, 15,
TMZ 10, 27
Tramm, Boris 62, 63
Tyumen 13, 21, 22, 27

Ural 5, 23, 41-43, 47, 50-54, 72, 80, 92, 101,
    103, 111, 118-120, 122

Vihur 84
VMPZ 44
Vneshposyltorg 47, 65
Voase, Alan 49, 121
Voskhod 32, 46, 47, 51, 52, 54, 65, 73, 99,
    104, 119, 120
Vostok (racers) 64, 73

Wall of Death 56, 109
Wells, Fred 47
Women 19, 54, 63, 84, 85, 87, 101, 109,
    121, 122,

Za Rulem 99, 106
Zapchastexport 45, 46
ZID 11, 19, 41
Znachki 78, 110
Zschopau 14, 26, 28, 30
Zundapp 11, 19